ideals®

P9-APB-061

Sophie Kay's
MICROWAVE
COOKBOOK

Ideals Publishing Corp.
Milwaukee, Wisconsin

CONTENTS _____

ISBN 0-8249-3022-3

Copyright © MCMLXXXIV by Ideals Publishing Corporation.
All rights reserved.
Printed and bound in the United States of America.

Published by Ideals Publishing Corporation.
11315 Watertown Plank Road
Milwaukee, WI 53226
Published simultaneously in Canada.

TIPS AND TECHNIQUES

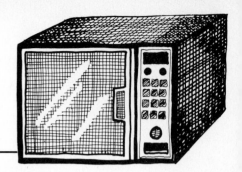

I have written this microwave cookbook with the experienced microwave cook in mind. For any newcomers, however, following is a brief explanation of a few of the techniques required for microwave cooking.

Power Settings

All microwave ovens function in essentially the same fashion; but manufacturers vary the design of the control panel. In an effort to keep these recipes as easy to use as possible and yet be applicable to all units, the following recipes indicate only high, medium or low power settings. On ovens which have numbered settings high, medium or low should be interpreted as percentages. For example, high is equivalent to one hundred percent for whichever type oven you are using. Some experimentation and familiarity with the operation of the oven may be required to adapt the high, medium and low settings.

Timing

When cooking with a microwave, timing is critical to the result and is affected by several things including size, density and moisture content of the food and the number of items in the oven. In addition, cooking time is affected by the starting temperature. For instance, food taken directly from the refrigerator will require longer cooking time than food which is at room temperature.

The recipes contained in this book give a range of time for cooking in addition to a recognizable doneness factor. For example, the instructions might say, "Microwave on high 5 to 6 minutes, or until golden." Because a microwave cooks in about one-third the time of conventional methods, a few seconds can make a big difference to the finished product. When preparing these recipes, begin checking for doneness at the minimum cooking time indicated.

Standing Time

Standing time is necessary to complete the cooking of many types of foods, such as roasts, cakes and egg dishes. Standing time enables heat to be conducted from the outside to the center of the food, thus completing the cooking process. During standing time, the dish or casserole may be left in the oven. If you are going to use the oven immediately for another recipe, however, remove the dish to a heat-resistant surface for its standing time. The standing time has been included in the Cooking Time listed at the beginning of each recipe. This gives an accurate idea of the total time required to prepare the recipe.

Utensils

Almost any material except metal is safe to use in a microwave oven. Ovenproof, ceramic or pottery dishes may be used, provided they have no metal trim or parts. Use plastic ware only for short periods of reheating.

Metal utensils, however, should not be used in a microwave oven. Metal reflects microwaves, thus preventing them from passing through the container and through the food. In addition, metal causes electricity to "arc," or spark, which can cause damage to the oven. The exception to this rule is in shielding food with small pieces of aluminum foil. (See Shielding.)

Covering Food

If the dish does not have a fitted lid, cover it instead with plastic wrap in which a few slits have been cut. These vents prevent the steam from building up and the food boiling over.

Browning Dishes

Browning dishes have a surface that becomes extremely hot when preheated in a microwave oven. These dishes can be used for foods that require a short cooking time and would not otherwise brown if prepared in a microwave, such as steaks or hamburgers. Stir-fried foods also brown nicely in a browing dish. In the following recipes, the preheating time for the browning dish has been included in the Cooking Time listed at the beginning of each recipe. This gives an accurate idea of total preparation time.

Shielding

When cooking large, dense foods such as roasts, whole chicken or turkey, shielding prevents areas of lesser density, such as drumsticks and wings, from drying out. Wrap a small piece of aluminum foil around the area to be shielded, according to the recipe instructions.

Shielding also helps cakes and cookies bake evenly. Wrap small strips of foil around the edges of the baking dish. This will prevent the outside edges of the cake or cookies from browning too rapidly. Foil, however, should never touch the oven walls.

Arranging the Food

Microwaves cook from the outside edges of the food inward. Food of higher density, therefore, should be arranged around the outer edge of the dish. For example, place chicken drumsticks in a dish with the tapered tip of the leg pointing toward the center of the dish. Elongated foods such as whole potatoes, should be arranged as spokes on a wheel; rounded foods such as cupcakes can be placed in a circle.

Turning Over

Roasts and whole poultry or other large and heavy foods must be turned completely over so that they will brown evenly and cook thoroughly. Recipes in this book indicate at what point food needs to be turned over.

Stirring

In microwave cooking, stirring is important to a successful end product because it distributes the heat for even cooking. Stir food from the outside of the dish toward the center. Recipes in this book will indicate at what point food needs to be stirred.

Rearranging

Solid foods that cannot be stirred must be rearranged in the dish. Recipes in this book will indicate when it is necessary to move the food from the center of the dish to the outside and the food on the outside to the center. Arrange the thicker portions of each piece toward the outside of the dish.

Rotating the Dish

If food cannot be stirred or rearranged, the dish must be rotated during the cooking time. This is especially important when baking; otherwise, cakes, breads, etc., may rise unevenly. Rotating will also aid the cooking of large, dense foods which require a longer cooking time. Recipes in this book indicate at which point in the cooking process it is necessary to rotate the dish. To rotate, turn the dish one-half turn. (Six o'clock will move to twelve o'clock position.)

Timing Adjustment

I developed and tested my recipes in a 600 to 700-watt microwave oven. For preparing these recipes in a 400 to 500-watt microwave oven, it will be necessary to increase cooking time by fifty percent. If using a 500 to 600-watt microwave oven, cooking time will increase by only twenty-five percent.

High Altitude Adjustments

Generally speaking, if using these recipes in high altitude locations, the cooking time will increase by approximately thirty percent.

I have been cooking and experimenting with my microwave for several years and love using it more each year. I hope you enjoy preparing the recipes in this book as much as I have enjoyed developing them. The microwave, with its ability to cook foods so much quicker than conventional ovens, adds to the fun of cooking. Enjoy!

OFF TO A GREAT START

Hot Crab Meat Dip

Makes 1½ cups   Cooking Time: 2 minutes

1 package (8 ounces) cream cheese, room temperature
2 teaspoons prepared horseradish
2 tablespoons minced onion
¼ teaspoon salt
Dash garlic powder

½ teaspoon Worcestershire sauce
3 to 4 drops hot pepper sauce
3 tablespoons chablis
1 can (6½ ounces) crab meat, well drained
½ teaspoon minced fresh *or* dried dillweed

In a medium bowl, combine cream cheese, horseradish, onion, salt, garlic powder, Worcestershire and hot pepper sauces. Microwave on HIGH 1 minute. Stir in chablis and crab meat. Microwave on HIGH 1 minute. Sprinkle dillweed over top and serve.

Rye Rounds

Makes 2 dozen   Cooking Time: 60 to 80 seconds

2 ounces Swiss cheese, shredded (½ cup)
3 tablespoons mayonnaise
1 tablespoon minced parsley

1 tablespoon minced onion
Dash cayenne pepper
24 rye melba toast rounds

In a medium bowl, combine all ingredients, except toast rounds. Spread a scant teaspoonful cheese mixture on each round. Arrange 12 rounds on a 12-inch microsafe plate. Microwave on MEDIUM 30 to 40 seconds or until cheese melts. Serve immediately. Repeat with remaining 12 rounds.

Pizza-Swiss Melts

Makes 2 dozen   Cooking Time: 3 to 4 minutes

4 ounces Swiss cheese, shredded (1 cup)
3 tablespoons grated Parmesan cheese
2 tablespoons pizza sauce
1 tablespoon mayonnaise

1 tablespoon minced chives
24 melba toast rounds
Sliced black olives

In a small bowl, combine cheeses, pizza sauce, mayonnaise, and chives; blend well. Spread about 1 teaspoon cheese mixture on each toast round. Arrange 12 rounds on a 12-inch microsafe plate. Microwave on LOW 1 minute. Rotate the plate. Microwave on LOW 30 seconds to 1 minute or until cheese melts. Garnish with sliced black olives. Repeat with remaining 12 rounds.

APPETIZERS

Creamy Beef Spread

Makes about 2 cups   Cooking Time: 4 to 6 minutes

- 1 package (8 ounces) cream cheese, room temperature
- 1 jar *or* package (2½ ounces) sliced dried beef, finely chopped (about ¾ cup)
- 2 tablespoons instant minced onion
- 2 tablespoons minced green pepper
- ⅛ teaspoon black pepper
- ½ cup dairy sour cream
- ¼ cup finely chopped pecans
- Assortment of crackers

In a medium bowl, combine cream cheese, dried beef, onion, green pepper, and pepper; blend well. Blend in sour cream. Spoon into an 8-inch microsafe pie plate. Sprinkle pecans over top. Microwave on MEDIUM 4 to 6 minutes or until hot. Serve immediately with crackers.

Guacamole Rounds

Makes 3 dozen   Cooking Time: 6 to 7½ minutes

- 2 ripe avocados, peeled, seeded, and mashed
- 1 medium tomato, chopped
- 1 medium onion, minced
- 1 tablespoon lemon juice
- ¼ teaspoon hot pepper sauce
- 36 round tortilla chips (about 2 inches diameter)
- 3 ounces Monterey Jack cheese, shredded (¾ cup)

In a medium bowl, combine avocados, tomato, onion, lemon juice, and hot pepper sauce; blend well. Place 1 teaspoonful on each tortilla chip. Sprinkle about 1 teaspoonful cheese on top of each round. Arrange 12 chips on a 12-inch microsafe plate. Microwave on MEDIUM 2 to 2½ minutes or until cheese melts. Serve immediately. Repeat with remaining chips, cooking 12 at a time.

Crab Roll-Ups

Makes about 30   Cooking Time: 9 to 11 minutes

- 1 can (6½ ounces) crab meat, drained and chopped
- ½ cup soft bread crumbs
- 1 tablespoon dry sherry
- 2 tablespoons minced chives
- ½ teaspoon dry mustard
- Dash salt
- Dash white pepper
- 6 bacon slices, cut crosswise in thirds

In a medium bowl, combine crab meat, bread crumbs, sherry, chives, mustard, salt, and pepper; blend well. Chill about 30 minutes. Shape into rolls, using 1 tablespoon crab meat mixture for each. Wrap a bacon piece around each roll; secure with wooden picks. Preheat a 10-inch microwave browning dish on HIGH 5 minutes. Immediately place rolls in dish. Microwave on HIGH 2 minutes. Turn rolls over and rearrange. Microwave on HIGH 2 to 4 minutes or until bacon is crisp. Drain on paper towels. Serve hot.

Stuffed Mushrooms

Makes about 18   Cooking Time: about 6½ minutes

- 12 ounces medium mushrooms
- 2 teaspoons butter
- 1 tablespoon minced chives
- 1 package (3 ounces) cream cheese, cut in pieces
- ⅛ teaspoon garlic powder
- ⅛ teaspoon salt
- Dash cayenne pepper
- Paprika

Remove stems from mushrooms with the tip of a knife; reserve mushroom caps. Finely chop stems. In a small microsafe baking dish, combine stems, butter, and chives. Microwave on HIGH 3 minutes or until mushrooms are tender, stirring after 1½ minutes. Add cream cheese. Microwave on HIGH 30 to 40 seconds or until cream cheese is softened. Add garlic powder, salt, and cayenne; blend well. Spoon mixture into centers of mushroom caps. Arrange on a paper towel-lined 12-inch microsafe plate. Microwave on HIGH 3 minutes or until mushrooms are hot. Sprinkle paprika lightly over mushrooms. Serve immediately.

Pizza Joes

Makes 8 to 12 servings   Cooking Time: 13 to 16 minutes

- 1 pound lean ground beef
- 1 medium onion, chopped
- 1 can (8 ounces) tomato sauce
- 1 can (4 ounces) sliced mushrooms, drained
- ¼ cup catsup
- 1 teaspoon salt
- ⅛ teaspoon black pepper
- 1 teaspoon crushed leaf oregano
- ¼ teaspoon crushed leaf basil
- ¼ teaspoon garlic powder
- 2 teaspoons Worcestershire sauce
- ⅛ teaspoon hot pepper sauce
- 4 ounces mozzarella cheese, grated (1 cup)
- 4 to 6 hamburger buns, halved and toasted

In a 2-quart microsafe casserole, crumble ground beef; add onion. Microwave on HIGH 7 to 9 minutes or until beef is no longer pink, stirring and breaking up beef every 2 minutes. Remove from oven; drain fat. Stir in tomato sauce, mushrooms, catsup, salt, pepper, oregano, basil, garlic powder, and Worcestershire and hot pepper sauces. Microwave on HIGH 4 to 5 minutes, stirring after 2 minutes. Sprinkle cheese evenly over top. Cover. Microwave on MEDIUM 2 minutes or until cheese melts. Spoon onto bottoms of buns; cover with tops of buns. Serve immediately.

Saucy Hot Dogs

Makes 8 to 10 servings   Cooking Time: 2½ to 4 minutes

- ¼ cup red currant jelly
- 1½ teaspoons Dijon mustard
- 1 pound frankfurters, diagonally cut in thirds

In a 1-quart microsafe casserole, combine jelly and mustard. Add frankfurters; stir lightly. Cover. Microwave on HIGH 2½ to 4 minutes or until bubbly and hot, stirring every 1½ minutes.

Nutty Cheese Ball

Makes 8 servings

Cooking Time: 2 to 3 minutes

1 teaspoon butter
¼ cup chopped green onion
1 clove garlic, pressed
**1 package (8 ounces) cream cheese,
   room temperature**
**6 ounces Cheddar cheese, shredded
   (1½ cups)**

2 tablespoons prepared horseradish
2 teaspoons Worcestershire sauce
¼ teaspoon hot pepper sauce
**1 tablespoon chopped pimiento,
   well drained**
⅓ cup finely chopped pecans
Assortment of crackers

In a small microsafe bowl, combine butter, green onion, and garlic. Cover with waxed paper. Microwave on HIGH 1 to 2 minutes or until onion is tender, stirring once during cooking time. In a separate large microsafe bowl, place cream cheese. Microwave on MEDIUM 50 to 60 seconds or until cream cheese is softened. Stir in onion mixture, Cheddar cheese, horseradish, and Worcestershire and hot pepper sauces. Using an electric mixer, beat cheese mixture on low speed until well blended. Beat on medium speed until fluffy. Stir in pimiento. Cover and chill 1 hour. Shape into a ball. Cover cheese ball with plastic wrap. Chill 2 to 3 hours. Remove plastic wrap. Roll in pecans to cover completely. Serve with crackers.

Toasty Nuts

Makes about 1½ cups

Cooking Time: 4½ to 5½ minutes

1 tablespoon butter
¼ teaspoon garlic salt
1 teaspoon Worcestershire sauce
¼ teaspoon hot pepper sauce

1 can (6 ounces) mixed nuts
**1 package (4 ounces) salted blanched
   peanuts**

In a 1-quart microsafe casserole, place butter. Microwave on HIGH 20 to 30 seconds or until butter melts. Stir in garlic salt and Worcestershire and hot pepper sauces. Add both nuts; toss to coat well. Microwave on HIGH 4 to 5 minutes or until butter is absorbed, stirring every 1½ minutes. Spread in a single layer on a paper towel-lined baking sheet. Let stand until dry. Store in an airtight container.

Crunchy Corn

Makes about 9 cups

Cooking Time: 12 to 15 minutes

1 cup butter
½ cup light corn syrup
1¼ cups sugar

2 quarts popped corn
1 cup salted blanched peanuts

In a 2½-quart microsafe bowl, combine butter, corn syrup, and sugar. Microwave on HIGH 12 to 15 minutes or until brittle threads form when a small amount is dropped into cold water, stirring every 3 minutes. Combine corn and nuts in a 6-quart container. Pour syrup evenly over corn mixture. Stir with 2 wooden spoons until popcorn mixture is well coated. Spread in a single layer on 2 large nonstick baking sheets. Let stand until firm. Break into small pieces. Store in an airtight container.

SNACKS

TV Snack Mix

Makes about 6 cups   Cooking Time: 4½ to 7½ minutes

2 cups thin pretzel sticks
1 can (3 ounces) chow mein noodles
(2 cups)
1 cup corn cereal squares
1½ cups Spanish peanuts

6 tablespoons butter
1 tablespoon Worcestershire sauce
½ teaspoon hot pepper sauce
1 teaspoon chili powder

In a large bowl, combine pretzels, chow mein noodles, corn cereal, and peanuts; set aside. In a separate small microsafe bowl, combine butter, Worcestershire and hot pepper sauces, and chili powder. Microwave on HIGH 1½ to 2½ minutes or until butter melts; stir to blend. Pour over pretzel mixture; toss to coat. Microwave on HIGH 3 to 5 minutes or until mixture is hot, stirring every 1 minute. Spread on paper towels. Cool completely before storing in an airtight container.

Nachos with Salsa

Makes 1 dozen   Cooking Time: 1 minute

12 round tortilla chips (about 2 inches
diameter)
2 ounces Cheddar *or* Monterey Jack
cheese, shredded (½ cup)

2 tablespoons taco seasoning mix
1 tablespoon water
½ cup taco sauce

On a paper towel-lined microsafe plate, place tortilla chips. In a small bowl, combine cheese, seasoning mix, and water. Top each chip with about 1 rounded teaspoonful cheese mixture. Microwave on HIGH 30 seconds. Rotate the plate. Microwave on HIGH 30 seconds. Serve hot, dipped in taco sauce.

Grapefruit Delight

Makes 4 servings   Cooking Time: 2½ to 4 minutes

2 large grapefruit, halved and sectioned
4 teaspoons brown sugar

4 teaspoons butter
2 maraschino cherries, halved

In an 8-inch microsafe baking dish or individual dishes, arrange grapefruit. Sprinkle 1 teaspoon brown sugar over each grapefruit half; top each with 1 teaspoon butter. Microwave on HIGH 2½ to 4 minutes, rotating the baking dish once during cooking time. Top each grapefruit half with a cherry half. Serve.
Note: A single serving of 1 grapefruit half will heat in about 1 minute.

Variation

Combine ¼ cup dairy sour cream and 3 tablespoons brown sugar. Spread over grapefruit halves before heating.

Mulled Cider

Makes 4 servings   Cooking Time: 10 to 12 minutes

3 tablespoons brown sugar   4 whole allspice
1 cinnamon stick   1 quart apple cider
4 whole cloves   4 thin orange slices, optional

In a 2-quart microsafe bowl, combine all ingredients, except orange slices. Microwave on
HIGH 10 to 12 minutes or until boiling. Strain to remove spices. Serve hot or chilled over ice.
Garnish with orange slices, if desired.

Hot Vege-Cocktail

Makes 2 to 3 servings   Cooking Time: 5 to 6 minutes

1 can (12 ounces) vegetable juice cocktail   Dash hot pepper sauce
1 teaspoon lemon juice   2 to 3 ribs celery (each about 6 inches
½ teaspoon Worcestershire sauce   long)

In a 1-quart glass measure, combine all ingredients, except celery. Microwave on HIGH 5 to 6
minutes or until bubbly. Pour into mugs. Place a celery rib in each mug and serve.

Hot Cocoa

Makes 2 to 3 servings   Cooking Time: 3 to 4¾ minutes

3 tablespoons unsweetened cocoa   1¾ cups milk
3 tablespoons sugar   ¼ teaspoon vanilla
¼ cup hot water   3 large marshmallows

In a 1-quart glass measure, combine cocoa and sugar. Add water; blend until smooth.
Microwave on HIGH 50 seconds to 1¼ minutes or until boiling. Stir in milk. Microwave on
HIGH 2 to 3½ minutes or until thoroughly heated. Stir in vanilla. Beat with a wire whisk until
foamy. Pour into mugs. Top each serving with a marshmallow.

Amaretto Café

Makes 3 to 4 servings   Cooking Time: 8 to 9 minutes

2½ cups water   3 ounces Amaretto liqueur
1 cup milk   Sweetened whipped cream
1½ tablespoons sugar   Cinnamon
3 rounded teaspoons instant coffee
   granules

In a 2-quart microsafe bowl, combine water, milk, sugar, and coffee granules. Microwave on
HIGH 8 to 9 minutes or until boiling. Stir in liqueur. Pour into mugs. Top each serving with
whipped cream. Sprinkle cinnamon on top and serve.

SOUP AND SANDWICH SAMPLER

Beefy Vegetable Soup

Makes 2 quarts

Cooking Time: 36 to 41 minutes

4 cups beef broth
1 cup chopped celery
1 small potato, peeled and cubed
1 cup chopped tomato, with juice
¼ cup chopped onion
¼ cup tomato sauce

¼ cup chopped carrot
3 tablespoons quick-cooking barley
2 tablespoons broken thin spaghetti
½ teaspoon salt
¼ teaspoon garlic powder
⅛ teaspoon black pepper

In a 3-quart microsafe casserole, pour broth. Cover. Microwave on HIGH 6 to 9 minutes or until boiling. Add remaining ingredients. Cover. Microwave on HIGH 5 minutes, stirring every 2 minutes. Microwave on HIGH 25 to 30 minutes or until vegetables are tender.

Barley Soup

Makes 6 servings

Cooking Time: 30½ to 31½ minutes

5 cups hot water
1 cup quick-cooking barley
2 tablespoons butter

½ teaspoon dried mint
1 cup dairy sour cream

In a 2-quart microsafe casserole, pour water. Cover. Microwave on HIGH 8 to 9 minutes or until boiling. Stir in barley. Cover. Microwave on HIGH 5 minutes. Remove cover. Microwave on HIGH 5 minutes; stir. Microwave on MEDIUM 10 minutes or until barley is tender. In a 1-cup glass measure, place butter. Microwave on HIGH 20 to 30 seconds. Stir in mint. Microwave on HIGH 2 minutes or until butter is just brown. Stir into barley mixture; set aside. In a small bowl, stir sour cream until creamy. Gradually stir about 1 cup soup into sour cream. Return sour cream mixture to soup; blend well. Serve warm or chilled. To reheat, microwave on LOW but do not boil.

Tomato Consommé

Makes about 4 servings

Cooking Time: 8 to 9 minutes

3 cups tomato juice
1 can (10½ ounces) condensed beef consommé
½ teaspoon celery salt
½ teaspoon crushed leaf thyme

¼ teaspoon seasoned salt
¼ teaspoon sugar
⅛ teaspoon black pepper
⅛ teaspoon Worcestershire sauce
Lemon slices

In a 2-quart microsafe casserole, combine all ingredients, except lemon slices. Microwave on HIGH 8 to 9 minutes or until boiling. Garnish with lemon slices. Serve warm or chilled.

SOUPS

French Onion Soup

Makes 4 servings   Cooking Time: 22 to 27½ minutes

- **3 tablespoons butter**
- **3 medium onions, thinly sliced**
- **2 teaspoons flour**
- **1 can (10½ ounces) beef broth**
- **1 can (10½ ounces) water**
- **2 tablespoons dry white wine**

- **¼ teaspoon salt**
- **¼ teaspoon black pepper**
- **½ cup croutons**
- **4 ounces Gruyere *or* mozzarella cheese, shredded (1 cup)**

In a 2-quart microsafe casserole, place butter. Microwave on HIGH 20 to 30 seconds or until butter melts. Stir in onions. Microwave on HIGH 12 to 15 minutes or until onions are tender, stirring every 4 minutes. Stir in flour, broth, water, wine, salt, and pepper. Microwave on HIGH 7 to 9 minutes or until mixture thickens slightly and bubbles, stirring every 1 minute. Ladle into 4 soup bowls. Top each serving with croutons. Sprinkle cheese on top. Microwave on MEDIUM 2½ to 3 minutes or until cheese melts, rearranging bowls after 1½ minutes.

Clam Chowder

Makes 4 servings   Cooking Time: 19½ to 23½ minutes

- **¼ cup butter**
- **2 cups frozen southern-style hashed brown potatoes, thawed**
- **¼ cup chopped celery**
- **3 tablespoons chopped onion**
- **3 tablespoons flour**

- **3 cups milk**
- **1 teaspoon salt**
- **¼ teaspoon white pepper**
- **1 can (6½ ounces) chopped clams; reserve liquid**

In a 2-quart microsafe casserole, place butter. Microwave on HIGH 30 to 40 seconds or until butter melts. Add potatoes, celery, and onion; blend well. Microwave on HIGH 4 to 7 minutes or until onion is tender. Stir in flour. Microwave on HIGH 2 minutes. Slowly drizzle in milk. Add salt and pepper. Microwave on HIGH 12 to 13 minutes or until bubbly. Slowly stir in clams with liquid. Microwave on HIGH 1 minute or until heated through.

Egg-Lemon Soup

Makes 4 servings   Cooking Time: 13 to 17 minutes

- **3 cups chicken broth**
- **2 cups hot water**
- **1¼ cups quick-cooking rice**
- **¼ cup butter**
- **¼ teaspoon salt**

- **⅛ teaspoon white pepper**
- **3 eggs**
- **½ teaspoon flour**
- **3 tablespoons lemon juice**

In a 3-quart microsafe casserole, combine chicken broth and hot water. Microwave on HIGH 4 minutes. Stir in rice, butter, salt, and pepper. Microwave on HIGH 7 to 10 minutes or until rice is tender, stirring every 3 minutes. Let stand 2 to 3 minutes. In a medium bowl, combine eggs and flour; beat until thick. Drizzle in lemon juice, beating constantly. Gradually stir in 1½ cups broth. Slowly return egg-broth mixture to broth with rice, stirring constantly.

Main-Dish Meatball Soup

Makes 4 servings   Cooking Time: about 28 minutes

1 pound lean ground beef
⅓ cup quick-cooking rice
¼ cup chopped onion
2 eggs, slightly beaten
2 tablespoons minced parsley
1 clove garlic, pressed or minced
1 teaspoon salt
¼ teaspoon dillweed

⅛ teaspoon black pepper
3 cups hot water
1 medium potato, peeled and diced
3 eggs
1 teaspoon flour
3 tablespoons lemon juice
French bread slices

In a mixing bowl, combine ground beef, rice, onion, 2 beaten eggs, parsley, garlic, salt, dillweed, and pepper; blend well. Shape into 1-inch balls; set aside. In a 3-quart microsafe casserole, pour water. Cover. Microwave on HIGH 5 minutes or until boiling. Carefully add meatballs and potato to boiling water. Cover. Microwave on HIGH 5 minutes; stir. Remove cover. Microwave on HIGH 3 minutes; stir. Microwave on MEDIUM 15 minutes or until meatballs are no longer pink. In a medium bowl, combine 3 eggs and flour; beat until thick and light-colored. Drizzle in lemon juice, beating constantly. Gradually stir in 1½ cups hot broth. Slowly return egg-broth mixture to broth with meatballs, stirring constantly. Serve with sliced French bread.

Tomato Olé Soup

Makes 6 servings   Cooking Time: 19½ to 21½ minutes

1 can (14½ ounces) stewed tomatoes, chopped; reserve juice
1 can (16 ounces) garbanzo beans; reserve liquid
2 cups water
1 can (4 ounces) chopped green chilies

1½ teaspoons salt
½ teaspoon sugar
½ teaspoon chili powder
¼ cup butter
⅓ cup minced onion
3 tablespoons flour

In a 2-quart microsafe casserole, combine tomatoes with juice, garbanzo beans, and water. Cover. Microwave on HIGH 8 to 10 minutes or until boiling. Remove cover. Microwave on MEDIUM 6 minutes. Stir in chilies, salt, sugar, and chili powder. In a 1-quart glass measure, place butter. Microwave on HIGH 30 seconds or until butter melts. Stir in onion. Microwave on HIGH 4 to 5 minutes or until onion is tender. Stir in flour. Microwave on HIGH 1 to 2 minutes or until bubbly. Gradually stir 1 cup hot soup mixture into onion mixture; blend well. Slowly return onion mixture to soup; blend well.

SANDWICHES _____

Beef Biscuit Pies _____

Makes 5 servings   Cooking Time: 10 to 12 minutes

¼ pound lean ground beef
¼ cup thinly sliced onion
1 tablespoon minced parsley
¼ teaspoon dried dillweed
¼ teaspoon salt

Dash black pepper
1 package (7.5 ounces) refrigerated
 buttermilk biscuits
2 tablespoons butter

In a 1-quart microsafe casserole, crumble ground beef. Add onion. Microwave on HIGH 1 minute; stir. Microwave 1 to 3 minutes or until beef is no longer pink, stirring every 30 seconds; drain fat. Add parsley, dillweed, salt, and pepper; blend well. Slightly flatten each biscuit with palms of hands. Spoon beef mixture onto 5 of the biscuits. Cover with remaining 5 biscuits; pinch edges to seal. Preheat a 10-inch microwave browning dish on HIGH 5 minutes. Place butter in the dish; brush butter over the bottom. Immediately place beef pies in the dish . Let stand 10 seconds to brown; turn and brown the second side 15 seconds. Turn pies over. Microwave on HIGH 30 to 60 seconds or until puffy. Let stand 2 minutes and serve.

Mock Monte Cristo _____

Makes 2 sandwiches   Cooking Time: 45 to 60 seconds

4 slices frozen French toast
4 ounces thinly sliced cooked ham

2 thin slices Swiss cheese
½ cup strawberry-flavored yogurt, stirred

Prepare French toast as directed on package. Place 2 slices ham and 1 slice cheese on 2 slices French toast. Place on a paper towel-lined microsafe plate. Microwave on HIGH 45 to 60 seconds or until cheese melts. Cover each with remaining French toast. Serve with yogurt for dipping.

Hot Hoagie _____

Makes 2 sandwiches   Cooking Time: 1 to 2 minutes

4 tablespoons Italian dressing
2 French rolls (about 6½ inches long), cut
 lengthwise in half
½ cup shredded lettuce
2 slices brick cheese

2 thin ham slices
2 thin salami slices
2 thin bologna slices
4 thin tomato slices
4 thin onion slices

Drizzle 2 tablespoons dressing over cut sides of rolls. Arrange half of lettuce on bottom half of each roll. Top each with a slice of cheese, ham, salami, bologna, and 2 slices tomato and onion. Cover with top half of roll. Place sandwiches on a paper towel-lined microsafe plate. Cover with a paper towel. Microwave on HIGH 1 to 2 minutes or until cheese melts.

SANDWICHES

Tuna Dogs

Makes 4 sandwiches

Cooking Time: 5 to 8 minutes

1 can (6½ or 7 ounces) tuna, drained and flaked
½ cup chopped celery
2 tablespoons chopped pimiento-stuffed olives
1 tablespoon sweet pickle relish
2 tablespoons chopped onion

½ teaspoon salt
½ cup mayonnaise
2 ounces Cheddar cheese, shredded (½ cup)
2 hamburger buns, split and toasted
Paprika
Sliced ripe olives

In a small bowl, combine all ingredients, except buns, paprika, and ripe olives. Divide equally among bun halves. Place sandwiches on a paper towel-lined microsafe plate. Cover with a paper towel. Microwave on MEDIUM 5 to 8 minutes or until hot and bubbly. Sprinkle paprika and sliced ripe olives over sandwiches and serve.

Avocado Croissants

Makes 4 sandwiches

Cooking Time: 3 to 5 minutes

Avocado Spread
4 croissants, split lengthwise
4 thin slices roast beef

8 thin slices Swiss cheese
Tomato slices

Prepare Avocado Spread. Open croissants so that they are flat. Spread 2 teaspoons Avocado Spread on each half of croissants. Place 1 slice roast beef and 2 slices cheese on each. Place 2 of the sandwiches on a 12-inch microsafe plate. Microwave on MEDIUM 1½ to 2½ minutes or until cheese melts. Garnish with tomato slices. Repeat for remaining sandwiches. Serve immediately.

Avocado Spread

1 large ripe avocado, peeled and seeded
2 tablespoons butter, softened
1 tablespoon parsley flakes
1 tablespoon dried chives

½ teaspoon crushed leaf tarragon
1 tablespoon lemon juice
⅛ teaspoon seasoned salt

In a food processor or blender, puree avocado. In a small mixing bowl, combine puree and remaining ingredients; stir until smooth.

1-2-3 BREADS

English Muffin Loaves

Makes 2 loaves   Cooking Time: 31 to 36 minutes

4½ to 5 cups flour
2 packages (¼ ounce each) active dry yeast
1½ tablespoons sugar

2 teaspoons salt
2½ cups milk
¼ teaspoon baking soda
1 tablespoon warm water

In a large mixing bowl, combine 3 cups of the flour, yeast, sugar, and salt; set aside. Into a 1-quart glass measure, pour milk. Microwave on HIGH 2 minutes or until very warm (105 to 115° F.). Pour into flour mixture. Beat by hand or with an electric mixer until smooth. Stir in enough remaining flour to make a stiff batter. Cover and let rise in a warm, draft-free place 40 minutes or until doubled in bulk. Dissolve baking soda in water. Stir down batter. Add baking soda mixture; blend well. Spoon batter into 2 greased 9 x 5-inch microsafe loaf pans or 1½-quart soufflé dishes. Cover and let rise 40 minutes or until doubled in bulk. Uncover. Microwave, 1 loaf at a time, on HIGH 8½ to 11 minutes or until a toothpick inserted in the center comes out clean, rotating the pan after 4 minutes. Let stand 5 minutes. Turn out of the pan onto a wire rack to cool completely. To serve, slice and toast in conventional oven.

Mini Pecan Puffs

Makes 6 servings   Cooking Time: 4½ to 5 minutes

⅓ cup butter *or* margarine
½ cup firmly packed light brown sugar
½ cup chopped pecans

2 teaspoons water
1 teaspoon cinnamon
1 can (7.5 ounces) refrigerator biscuits

In an 8-inch microsafe pie plate, place butter and sugar. Microwave on HIGH 1 minute or until butter melts. Stir in pecans, water, and cinnamon. Separate biscuits; cut each into quarters. Place in butter mixture; stir to coat each piece. Arrange biscuits around outside of pie plate. Place a custard cup in the center of the pie plate. Microwave on HIGH 2½ to 3 minutes. Remove custard cup. Let stand 2 minutes before pulling puffs apart to serve.

Onion Cheese Bread

Makes 4 servings   Cooking Time: 5 minutes

1 cup thinly sliced onion
2 cloves garlic, minced
½ cup butter

⅓ cup minced parsley
½ cup grated Parmesan cheese
½ loaf French bread, split lengthwise

In a 1-quart microsafe bowl, combine onion, garlic, and butter. Cover with a paper towel. Microwave on HIGH 4 minutes. Stir in parsley. Microwave on HIGH 1 minute. Stir in cheese. Spread on bread halves. Serve immediately.

BREADS

Banana Nut Ring

Makes 12 servings   Cooking Time: 25 minutes

- 1 package (16 ounces) quick nut bread mix
- ¾ cup water
- 1 medium ripe banana, mashed
- 1 egg
- ¾ teaspoon cinnamon, divided
- ¼ cup finely chopped walnuts

Butter a 5-cup microsafe ring mold; set aside. In a medium mixing bowl, combine bread mix, water, banana, egg, and ½ teaspoon cinnamon; stir just until ingredients are moistened. In a small bowl, combine nuts and remaining ¼ teaspoon cinnamon. Sprinkle evenly over bottom and sides of prepared ring mold. Pour batter over nut mixture. Microwave on MEDIUM 15 minutes or until a wooden pick inserted in the center comes out clean, rotating the ring mold every 5 minutes. Let stand 10 minutes; invert onto a wire rack to cool before slicing.

Carrot Muffins

Makes about 11   Cooking Time: 11 minutes

- 1 egg
- ½ cup sugar
- ¼ cup vegetable oil
- 1 cup grated carrot
- 1¼ cups flour
- 1½ teaspoons baking powder
- 1 teaspoon pumpkin pie spice
- ½ teaspoon baking soda
- ⅛ teaspoon salt

In a medium mixing bowl, break egg; beat slightly. Add sugar, oil, and carrot; blend well. Add remaining ingredients. Stir just until dry ingredients are moistened. (The batter will be lumpy.) Spoon the batter into paper-lined microsafe muffin cups, filling each half full. Microwave on HIGH 1½ minutes. Rotate the muffin pan. Microwave on HIGH 1 minute. (The tops of the muffins will appear moist.) Let stand 3 minutes to finish cooking. Remove muffins from pan. Repeat with remaining batter.

Applesauce Muffins

Makes about 12   Cooking Time: about 9 minutes

- 1 tablespoon sugar
- 1 teaspoon cinnamon
- 1⅓ cups flour
- ½ cup firmly packed brown sugar
- 2 teaspoons baking powder
- ½ teaspoon salt
- ½ teaspoon cinnamon
- ¼ cup vegetable shortening
- ¾ cup applesauce
- ½ cup chopped nuts
- 2 eggs
- ¼ cup milk

In a small bowl, combine sugar and cinnamon; set aside. In a large mixing bowl, combine remaining ingredients. Stir just until dry ingredients are moistened. Spoon the batter into paper-lined microsafe muffin cups, filling each half full. Microwave on HIGH 1½ minutes. Rotate the muffin pan. Microwave on HIGH 60 to 70 seconds. (The tops of the muffins will appear moist.) Sprinkle half of sugar-cinnamon mixture over muffins. Let stand 2 minutes to finish cooking. Remove muffins from pan. Repeat with remaining batter and topping.

PRIZE-WINNING POULTRY

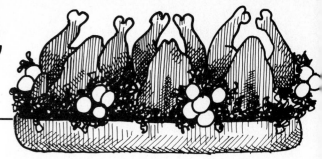

Basque Chicken

Makes 4 servings   Cooking Time: 50 to 63 minutes

- 3 tablespoons butter
- 1 broiler-fryer chicken (3 pounds), cut in 8 serving pieces
- 1½ cups finely chopped celery
- 1 cup finely chopped onions
- ¼ cup shredded carrot
- 1 small clove garlic, pressed
- 1 teaspoon salt
- ¼ teaspoon white pepper
- ½ teaspoon crushed leaf tarragon
- 1½ cups diced fresh tomatoes
- 1 can (8 ounces) tomato sauce
- ¼ cup tomato paste
- 1½ cups chicken broth
- 8 uncooked medium pasta shells
- Grated Parmesan cheese

In a 2½-quart microsafe casserole, place butter. Microwave on HIGH 40 to 50 seconds or until butter is deep brown. Make 2 slits in each piece of chicken. Arrange, skin side down, in butter with thickest portions toward the outside of the dish. Microwave on HIGH 10 minutes, rotating the casserole after 5 minutes. Turn chicken over and rearrange. Microwave on HIGH 10 minutes, rotating the dish after 5 minutes. Add celery, onions, carrot, garlic, salt, pepper, tarragon, tomatoes, tomato sauce, tomato paste, and chicken broth. Cover. Microwave on HIGH 9 to 11 minutes, rotating the dish after 5 minutes. (Chicken is done when pierced with a fork in the thickest portion and juices run clear.) Remove chicken; cover and set aside to keep warm. Add shells to vegetable mixture. Cover. Microwave on HIGH 5 to 8 minutes or until boiling, stirring every 2 minutes. Cover. Microwave on MEDIUM 10 to 15 minutes or until shells are tender, stirring every 5 minutes. Arrange chicken on top of shells; baste with broth. Cover. Microwave on MEDIUM 5 to 8 minutes or until chicken is hot. Let stand, covered, 5 minutes. Sprinkle Parmesan cheese on top and serve.

Chicken with 25 Cloves of Garlic

Makes 4 to 6 servings   Cooking Time: 27 to 30 minutes

- 1 teaspoon salt
- ¼ teaspoon black pepper
- 1 roasting chicken (4 to 5 pounds)
- ¼ teaspoon crushed leaf thyme
- ⅛ teaspoon crushed leaf oregano
- 4 thin lemon slices
- 25 whole unpeeled cloves garlic
- 1 tablespoon olive oil
- Paprika
- Sliced French bread

Sprinkle salt and pepper over chicken; rub into skin. Rub thyme and oregano inside body cavity. Tie legs and wings to bird with string. Place chicken, breast down, in a 3-quart microsafe casserole. Arrange lemon slices and garlic around chicken. Drizzle oil evenly over chicken. Sprinkle paprika lightly over skin. Cover. Microwave on HIGH 10 minutes, rotating the dish after 5 minutes. Turn chicken, breast up. Rotate the dish in oven; cover. Microwave on HIGH 12 to 15 minutes, rotating the dish after 6 minutes. (Chicken is done when pierced with a fork in the thickest part of the breast and juices run clear.) Let stand 5 minutes. Place chicken and garlic on a serving platter. Serve French bread spread with garlic cloves.

Roast Duckling with Cherry Glaze

Makes 2 servings   Cooking Time: 45 to 55 minutes

1 frozen duckling (4½ to 5 pounds), thawed

2 tablespoons soy sauce
Cherry Glaze

Using a fork, pierce the skin well. Twist wing tips behind back. Secure neck skin to back with wooden picks, covering wing tips. Tie legs and wings to bird with string. Brush skin well with soy sauce. Place duckling, breast down, in a microsafe roasting pan or on a microwave rack in a 12 x 7-inch microsafe baking dish. Cover with a tent of greased waxed paper. Microwave on HIGH 15 minutes, rotating the baking dish every 5 minutes. Remove from oven; drain fat. Prepare Cherry Glaze. Brush duckling with glaze. Turn duckling, breast up. Rotate the baking dish. Cover with greased waxed paper. Microwave on HIGH 25 to 35 minutes, rotating the baking dish every 12 minutes and brushing with glaze. (Duckling is done when pierced with a fork between the leg and thigh and juices run clear or when the temperature is 185° F. on a microwave meat thermometer inserted between the leg and thigh.) Remove from oven; drain fat. Brush with glaze. Cover tightly with aluminum foil. Let stand 5 minutes. Pass remaining glaze with duckling.

Cherry Glaze

Makes about ¾ cup   Cooking Time: 1 minute

½ cup cherry preserves
¼ cup sugar

1 teaspoon lemon juice
¼ teaspoon ginger

In a 1-cup glass measure, combine all ingredients. Microwave on HIGH 1 minute or until warm.

Turkey Couscous

Makes 4 to 6 servings   Cooking Time: 36½ to 42½ minutes

2 cups bulgur *or* cracked wheat
¼ cup butter
½ cup chopped onion
¼ cup diced carrot
¼ cup diced green pepper
3 cups chicken broth
1 cup peeled chopped tomato

2 teaspoons salt
⅛ teaspoon cayenne pepper
Pinch allspice
3 cups diced cooked turkey
1 cup frozen peas, thawed
Minced parsley

Rinse bulgur in warm water; drain well; set aside. In a 2-quart microsafe casserole, place butter. Microwave on HIGH 30 to 40 seconds or until butter melts. Add onion, carrot, and green pepper. Microwave on HIGH 2 minutes, stirring after 1 minute. Pour in chicken broth. Cover. Microwave on HIGH 5 to 8 minutes or until mixture boils. Stir in bulgur, tomato, salt, cayenne, and allspice. Cover. Microwave on HIGH 4 to 5 minutes or until boiling. Microwave on HIGH 10 minutes, stirring every 3 minutes. Stir in turkey and peas. Cover. Microwave on MEDIUM 10 to 12 minutes or until bulgur is tender and water is absorbed. Let stand, covered, 5 minutes. Garnish with parsley and serve.

Step-by-step:
Turkey Breast with Vegetables

1. Melted butter, prepared vegetables and seasonings.
2. Basted turkey breast in microsafe baking dish with tent of greased waxed paper.
3. Vegetables added to microsafe baking dish with turkey breast; turkey breast is basted again.
4. Microwave meat thermometer can be inserted at this point; turkey breast will be done when temperature reaches 185° F.
5. Golden Turkey Breast with Vegetables is ready for dining enjoyment and rave reviews.

1.

2.

3.

4.

5.

Cantonese Stir-Fry

Makes 4 servings

Cooking Time: about 11 minutes

¼ cup soy sauce
2 tablespoons vegetable oil
1 clove garlic, minced
3 thin slices gingerroot
2 whole boned and skinned chicken breasts, cut in ¾ x 1½-inch strips

1 large green pepper, cut in ½-inch strips
½ cup sliced water chestnuts
1 medium onion, cut in thin slices and separated into rings
Fluffy hot rice

In a medium bowl, combine soy sauce, oil, garlic, and gingerroot. Add chicken strips; stir to coat chicken. Let stand 30 minutes. Preheat a 10-inch microwave browning dish on HIGH 5 minutes. Immediately add chicken with marinade, green pepper, and water chestnuts. Stir until sizzling stops. Stir in onion. Microwave on HIGH 2 minutes. Stir. Cover with plastic wrap. Microwave on HIGH 4 minutes or until chicken is tender, stirring after 2 minutes. Serve with hot rice.

Turkey Breast With Vegetables

Makes 6 to 8 servings

Cooking Time: 1 hour 51 minutes

6 tablespoons butter, divided
4 cups diagonally sliced celery
1 cup chopped onions
8 ounces fresh mushrooms, sliced
2 cups thinly sliced carrots
1 package (10 ounces) frozen broccoli spears, thawed
2 medium potatoes, peeled and cut in large cubes

¼ cup minced parsley
½ teaspoon salt
½ teaspoon garlic powder
¾ teaspoon black pepper, divided
1 tablespoon lemon juice
2 teaspoons paprika
1 frozen whole turkey breast (4 to 5 pounds), thawed and trimmed
Salt, optional

In a large microsafe bowl, place 4 tablespoons butter. Microwave on HIGH 30 to 40 seconds or until butter melts. Add celery, onions, mushrooms, carrots, broccoli, potatoes, parsley, salt, garlic powder, and ¼ teaspoon pepper; blend well; set aside. In a 1-cup glass measure, place remaining 2 tablespoons butter. Microwave on HIGH 20 to 30 seconds or until butter melts. Stir in lemon juice, paprika, and remaining ½ teaspoon pepper. Tie back section of turkey breast, if necessary. Secure neck skin to back with wooden picks. Place breast, skin side down, in a 12 x 7-inch microsafe baking dish. Brush on lemon-butter mixture. Cover with a tent of greased waxed paper. Microwave on HIGH 15 minutes, rotating the baking dish every 5 minutes. Remove breast from baking dish; set aside. Arrange vegetables in baking dish. Place breast, skin side up, on top of vegetables. Brush on lemon-butter mixture. Cover with waxed paper. Microwave on MEDIUM 90 minutes, rotating the baking dish and basting with lemon-butter every 25 minutes. (Turkey breast is done when pierced with a fork in the thickest part of the breast and juices run clear or when the temperature is 185° F. on a microwave meat thermometer.) Brush breast with remaining lemon-butter mixture. Sprinkle with salt to taste, if desired. Cover tightly with aluminum foil. Let stand on a heat-resistant surface 5 minutes before serving.

POULTRY _____

Glazed Cornish Hens _____

Makes 4 servings   Cooking Time: 37 to 39 minutes

4 frozen Rock Cornish hens (1 to 1½   **Currant Glaze**
pounds each), thawed

Prepare Currant Glaze; set aside. Remove giblets from hens. Twist wing tips behind backs. Tie legs with string. Brush hens with Currant Glaze. Place hens, breast side down, in a 12 x 7-inch microsafe baking dish. Cover with a tent of greased waxed paper. Microwave on HIGH 16 minutes, rotating the dish after 8 minutes. Turn breast up and rotate the baking dish. Brush on glaze. Cover with a waxed paper tent. Microwave on HIGH 16 to 18 minutes, basting with glaze and rotating the baking dish after 8 minutes. (Hens are done when pierced with a fork between the leg and thigh and juices run clear.) Brush hens with glaze. Cover tightly with aluminum foil. Let stand 5 minutes before serving.

Currant Glaze

Makes about 1 cup   Cooking Time: 3½ to 4½ minutes

1 tablespoon butter   **2 teaspoons white vinegar**
⅔ cup red currant jelly   **1 tablespoon cornstarch**
¼ cup grenadine liqueur   **½ teaspoon salt**
2 tablespoons lemon juice, divided   **4 whole cloves**

In a 1-quart glass measure, place butter. Microwave on HIGH 20 seconds or until butter melts. Add jelly, grenadine, and 1 tablespoon lemon juice. Microwave on HIGH 1 to 2 minutes or until jelly melts. In a small bowl, combine remaining 1 tablespoon lemon juice, vinegar, cornstarch, salt, and cloves; blend well. Stir into jelly mixture. Microwave on HIGH 2 minutes or until mixture boils and thickens. Discard cloves before using.

Autumn Squash Supper _____

Makes 4 servings   Cooking Time: about 20 minutes

2 medium acorn squash (1 pound each)   **Dash ground cloves**
1 medium unpeeled apple, cored   **Dash ground cinnamon**
and diced   **2 tablespoons butter**
2 cups cubed cooked chicken   **⅓ cup chopped unsalted blanched**
1 tablespoon brown sugar   **peanuts**

Using a long metal skewer or sharp knife, pierce squash through to the center in several places. Place on a paper towel in microwave oven. Microwave on HIGH 5 minutes; turn over. Microwave on HIGH 5 minutes. Let stand 5 minutes. Cut in half vertically; discard seeds and fibers. Scoop out about ⅓ cup pulp from each half; set aside. In a medium bowl, combine apple, chicken, sugar, cloves, cinnamon, and pulp; blend well. Spoon apple filling into squash halves. Place halves in a large microsafe glass baking dish; dot with butter. Sprinkle peanuts over top. Cover with a paper towel. Microwave on HIGH 5 minutes or until squash is tender. Cover with aluminum foil. Let stand 5 minutes before serving.

PORK PLATTERS

Marmalade Ham Roast

Makes 6 to 8 servings   Cooking Time: about 1 hour 12 minutes

3 pounds fully cooked boneless
   smoked ham
   Whole cloves
¼ cup orange marmalade

2 tablespoons brown sugar
2 tablespoons sweet wine
½ teaspoon dry mustard

In a shallow 3-quart microsafe casserole, place ham, fat side down. Cover tightly with plastic wrap. Microwave on HIGH 7 minutes. Turn ham, fat side up. Score fat about ¼ inch deep in diamond pattern; insert cloves where points meet. Cover with plastic wrap. Microwave on MEDIUM 20 minutes. Remove from oven. Use wooden picks to secure small pieces of aluminum foil to edges of ham. Rotate the dish. Cover with plastic wrap. Microwave on MEDIUM 30 minutes, rotating the dish after 15 minutes. (Internal temperature should register 135° F. on a microwave meat thermometer inserted in the center of ham.) In a small bowl, combine remaining ingredients; blend well. Spread over ham. Cover with plastic wrap. Microwave on MEDIUM 5 minutes. Cover with aluminum foil. Let stand 10 minutes or until internal temperature registers 140° F. before serving.

Stuffed Pork Chops

Makes 4 servings   Cooking Time: 44 to 50½ minutes

2 tablespoons butter
1 teaspoon minced onion
3 tablespoons thinly sliced mushrooms
2 ounces blue cheese, crumbled (½ cup)
½ cup fine dry bread crumbs

4 center-cut pork chops (1 to 1½ inches
   thick), pockets slit in sides
1 package (¾ ounce) gravy mix for pork
1 cup water

In a small microsafe bowl, place butter. Microwave on HIGH 20 to 30 seconds. Add onion and mushrooms. Cover with waxed paper. Microwave on HIGH 1½ to 2 minutes. Stir blue cheese into mushroom mixture. Add bread crumbs; blend well. Fill pockets of pork chops with about ¼ cup stuffing. Secure with wooden picks. Place chops on a microwave rack in an 11 x 7-inch microsafe baking dish, stuffing side toward the outside of the dish. Cover with vented plastic wrap. Microwave on HIGH 5 minutes. Turn chops over. Microwave on MEDIUM 35 to 40 minutes or until chops are tender, turning chops over and rotating the baking dish after 15 minutes. (Chops are done when no longer pink in the center.) Remove chops to a warm platter; cover tightly with plastic wrap. Remove rack from the baking dish. Stir gravy mix and water into drippings. Microwave on HIGH 2 to 3 minutes or until thickened, stirring every 1 minute. Serve gravy with chops.

Barbecued Pork Ribs

Makes 2 to 3 servings   Cooking Time: 60 to 75 minutes

2 pounds country-style pork spareribs
Barbecue Sauce

On a microwave rack in a 12 x 7-inch microsafe baking dish, arrange ribs, bone side down, overlapping if necessary. Cover with vented plastic wrap. Microwave on HIGH 10 minutes, rotating the baking dish after 5 minutes. Rearrange ribs. Microwave on MEDIUM 30 to 40 minutes, rearranging ribs after 15 minutes. Pour Barbecue Sauce over ribs. Cover with vented plastic wrap. Microwave on MEDIUM 10 to 15 minutes or until heated through. Let stand, covered, 10 minutes before serving.

Barbecue Sauce
Makes about 1½ cups   Cooking Time: 3 to 5 minutes

1½ teaspoons cornstarch
½ cup water
1 can (6 ounces) tomato paste
2 tablespoons brown sugar
2 tablespoons chili sauce
2 tablespoons vegetable oil

2 tablespoons vinegar
1 tablespoon instant minced onion
1 teaspoon Worcestershire sauce
1 teaspoon salt
¼ teaspoon garlic powder
¼ teaspoon hot pepper sauce

In a 1-quart glass measure, blend cornstarch and 1 tablespoon water. Stir in remaining ingredients. Microwave on HIGH 3 to 5 minutes or until boiling.

Aloha Dinner

Makes 4 servings   Cooking Time: 19 to 21 minutes

1 tablespoon vegetable oil
1 cup sliced fresh mushrooms
½ cup cubed red pepper (¾-inch pieces)
½ cup cubed green pepper (¾-inch pieces)
1 package (6 ounces) frozen snow peas, thawed
1 clove garlic, minced
1 can (8 ounces) pineapple chunks, drained; reserve juice

½ cup chicken broth
3 tablespoons honey
2 tablespoons soy sauce
2 tablespoons lemon juice
3 tablespoons cornstarch
1 slice (about ½ pound) fully cooked ham, cut in 1½ x ¾-inch strips
Hot cooked rice

Preheat a 10-inch microwave browning dish on HIGH 5 minutes. Place oil, mushrooms, pepper, snow peas, and garlic in the dish; stir until sizzling stops. Microwave on HIGH 4 minutes. In a small bowl, combine reserved pineapple juice, broth, honey, soy sauce, lemon juice, and cornstarch; blend well. Stir into mushroom mixture. Add ham and pineapple; blend well. Cover. Microwave on HIGH 7 to 10 minutes, stirring every 2 minutes. Let stand 3 minutes before serving over hot rice.

PORK

Glazed Pork Loin

Makes 6 servings   Cooking Time: 1 hour 9 minutes to 1 hour 29 minutes

Orange Glaze
1 boneless pork loin roast (3 to 3½ pounds)

Prepare Orange Glaze; set aside. Place roast, fat side down, on a microwave rack in a 12 x 7-inch microsafe baking dish. Cover with a waxed paper tent. Microwave on HIGH 7 minutes. Turn roast fat side up. Rotate the baking dish. Cover with waxed paper. Microwave on HIGH 7 minutes. Use wooden picks to secure small pieces of aluminum foil to edges of roast. Cover with waxed paper. Microwave on MEDIUM 40 minutes, rotating the baking dish every 15 minutes. Turn roast over. Brush on Orange Glaze. Cover with waxed paper. Microwave on MEDIUM 10 to 20 minutes, rotating the baking dish every 5 minutes. (Internal temperature should register 165° F. on a microwave meat thermometer inserted in the center of roast.) Cover with a tent of aluminum foil. Let stand 15 minutes or until internal temperature registers 170° F. in several places. Slice and serve with remaining Orange Glaze.

Orange Glaze

Makes about 1 cup   Cooking Time: 3 minutes

⅓ **cup orange juice**   **1 tablespoon ground ginger**
½ **cup honey**   ¼ **teaspoon ground cloves**

In a small bowl, combine all ingredients. Microwave on HIGH 3 minutes; stir to blend.

Party Peaches with Ham

Makes 5 to 6 servings   Cooking Time: 19 to 22 minutes

1 can (16 ounces) sliced cling peaches,   **1 small clove garlic, pressed or minced**
drained; reserve ½ cup syrup   **1 slice (about 1 pound) fully cooked ham,**
¼ **cup water**   **cut in 2-inch julienne strips**
2 tablespoons dry sherry   ½ **cup thinly sliced green onion**
2 tablespoons soy sauce   ½ **cup thinly sliced celery**
1 tablespoon honey   **1 cup fresh or thawed frozen peas**
1 tablespoon cornstarch   **1 can (4½ ounces) sliced water**
¼ **teaspoon ground ginger**   **chestnuts, drained**
1 tablespoon peanut or vegetable oil   **Hot cooked rice or noodles**

In a medium bowl, combine peach syrup, water, sherry, soy sauce, honey, cornstarch, and ginger; set aside. Preheat a 10-inch microwave browning dish on HIGH 5 minutes. Place oil, garlic, ham, onion, and celery in the dish; stir 1 minute. Cover with waxed paper. Microwave on HIGH 4 minutes. Stir in cornstarch mixture. Cover with waxed paper. Microwave on HIGH 2 to 3 minutes or until thickened, stirring every 1 minute. Add peas and water chestnuts. Cover. Microwave on HIGH 2 to 3 minutes to heat through; stir. Arrange peaches on top. Cover. Microwave on HIGH 3 to 4 minutes or until hot. Let stand, covered, 2 minutes. Serve over rice or noodles.

BEEF BOUNTY

Classic Cabbage Rolls

Makes 4 servings
Cooking Time: 50 to 52 minutes

- 1 quart hot water
- 1 small cabbage, cored
- 1 pound lean ground beef
- ⅔ cup quick-cooking rice
- 1 medium onion, chopped
- 1 can (14½ ounces) stewed tomatoes, cut up; reserve juice
- ¼ cup minced parsley
- 1½ teaspoons dried dillweed
- 1 teaspoon salt
- ¼ teaspoon black pepper
- ¼ teaspoon garlic powder
- 1¼ cups water
- 2 tablespoons tomato paste
- 2 tablespoons butter

In a 3-quart microsafe casserole, pour 1 quart hot water. Cover. Microwave on HIGH 6 to 8 minutes or until boiling. Place cabbage, core side down, in boiling water. Microwave on HIGH 5 minutes. Turn cabbage, core side up. Microwave on HIGH 2 minutes. Remove cabbage from casserole. Remove leaves, 1 at a time. (If leaves are difficult to remove, microwave cabbage, core side down, on HIGH 3 to 4 minutes.) Cut center vein from each leaf; set leaves aside. In a large bowl, combine next 9 ingredients; blend well. Divide mixture evenly among centers of cabbage leaves. Fold sides of leaves in over meat mixture and roll up. In a 12 x 9-inch microsafe oval baking dish, place cabbage rolls, seam side down, in a single layer. Pour 1¼ cups water into a 1-quart glass measure. Microwave on HIGH 2 minutes or until boiling. Pour 1 cup water over cabbage rolls. Cover with plastic wrap. Microwave on HIGH 15 minutes or until boiling. Turn cabbage rolls over and rearrange by turning outside edges toward the center. Cover with vented plastic wrap. Microwave on HIGH 10 minutes. Stir into sauce. Stir tomato paste and butter into remaining ¼ cup water. Carefully stir into sauce. Turn rolls over and rearrange as before. Cover with plastic wrap. Microwave on HIGH 10 minutes or until tender.

Steak Sicilian

Makes 2 servings
Cooking Time: 8½ to 9½ minutes

- 2 strip steaks (about 1 inch thick)
- 4 teaspoons steak sauce
- ¼ cup grated Parmesan cheese

Use a sharp knife to slash steaks, 1 inch apart, on both sides. Preheat a 10-inch microwave browning dish on HIGH 5 minutes. Place steaks in the browning dish. For medium rare, microwave on HIGH 1½ minutes on first side. Turn steaks over. Microwave on HIGH 2 to 3 minutes on second side. During last 30 seconds, spread 2 teaspoons steak sauce on top of each steak. Sprinkle 2 tablespoons Parmesan cheese evenly over each steak. Serve immediately.

Note: For medium doneness, microwave on HIGH 2 minutes on first side; 3 to 4 minutes on second side.

BEEF

Lasagna

Makes 4 to 5 servings   Cooking Time: 49 to 56 minutes

- 1 pound lean ground beef
- 1 can (16 ounces) whole tomatoes, cut up; reserve juice
- 1 can (6 ounces) tomato paste
- ½ teaspoon salt
- ½ teaspoon crushed leaf basil
- 1 teaspoon crushed leaf oregano
- ⅛ teaspoon garlic powder

- ½ cup water
- ½ cup grated Parmesan cheese
- 2 cups small curd cottage cheese
- 1 egg, slightly beaten
- 2 tablespoons parsley flakes
- 8 uncooked lasagna noodles
- 8 ounces mozzarella cheese, shredded (2 cups)

In a 1½-quart microsafe baking dish, crumble ground beef. Microwave on HIGH 5 to 6 minutes or until beef is no longer pink, stirring every 2 minutes and breaking up beef; drain fat. Stir in tomatoes and juice, tomato paste, salt, basil, oregano, garlic powder, and water. Cover. Microwave on HIGH 4 to 5 minutes or until boiling, stirring every 2 minutes; set aside. In a medium bowl, combine Parmesan and cottage cheeses, egg, and parsley flakes; blend well. Spread 1½ cups tomato mixture in a 12 x 9-inch microsafe baking dish. Place 4 lasagna noodles in single layer over sauce. Spoon half of cottage cheese mixture on top; spread evenly. Sprinkle on half of mozzarella cheese. Pour 1 cup sauce evenly over cheese. Place remaining noodles over sauce. Top with layers of remaining cottage cheese mixture, mozzarella cheese, and sauce. Cover tightly with vented plastic wrap. Microwave on HIGH 15 minutes, rotating the baking dish every 5 minutes. Microwave on LOW 15 to 20 minutes or until noodles are tender, rotating the baking dish every 5 minutes. Let stand, covered, 10 minutes before serving.

Beefy Tostadas

Makes 8 servings   Cooking Time: 29 to 32 minutes

- 1 pound lean ground beef
- 2 cups chopped onions, divided
- 1 package (1¼ ounces) taco seasoning mix
- ¾ cup water
- 8 large corn tortillas

- 1 cup chopped tomatoes
- 2 cups shredded lettuce
- 4 ounces Cheddar cheese, shredded (1 cup)
- ½ cup sliced ripe olives, drained
- 1 jar (8 ounces) taco sauce

In a 1-quart microsafe casserole, crumble ground beef. Add 1 cup chopped onions. Microwave on HIGH 5 to 7 minutes or until beef is no longer pink, stirring every 1½ minutes and breaking up beef; drain fat. Add taco seasoning mix and water. Cover. Microwave on MEDIUM 10 minutes, stirring every 3 minutes. Let stand, covered, 10 minutes. Place 4 tortillas at a time on a paper towel-lined microsafe plate. (Do not overlap.) Microwave on HIGH 4 to 5 minutes or until crisp, turning tortillas over and rearranging every 1 minute. Divide beef mixture, remaining 1 cup chopped onions, tomatoes, lettuce, cheese, ripe olives, and taco sauce among tortillas. Serve immediately.

       Beefy Tostadas

BEEF

Bavarian Bologna Salad

Makes 4 servings   Cooking Time: 26 to 30 minutes

4 cups cubed, peeled potatoes (½-inch cubes)
2 cups hot water
1 cup mayonnaise
¼ cup grated onion
2 tablespoons minced parsley

2 tablespoons prepared mustard
2 tablespoons white wine vinegar
1 tablespoon sugar
½ teaspoon dried dillweed
⅛ teaspoon black pepper
1 pound ring bologna, cut in ¼-inch slices

In a 2-quart microsafe casserole, combine potatoes and water. Cover. Microwave on HIGH 14 to 16 minutes or until tender, stirring after 7 minutes. Let stand, covered, 2 minutes; drain. In a large bowl, combine mayonnaise, onion, parsley, mustard, vinegar, sugar, dillweed, and pepper; blend well. Add potatoes and bologna; blend well. Pour into a 9-inch microsafe pie plate. Cover with waxed paper. Microwave on MEDIUM 10 to 12 minutes or until heated through, rotating the pie plate every 4 minutes.

Corned Beef and Cabbage

Makes 4 servings   Cooking Time: about 1½ hours

1 corned beef brisket (about 3 pounds)
2 small cloves garlic, cut lengthwise in half
½ cup water
¼ cup dry white wine

2 medium potatoes, peeled and quartered
2 medium onions, quartered
3 small carrots, peeled and quartered
½ small head cabbage, cut in wedges

In a 4-quart microsafe casserole, place brisket, fat side down, with juices and seasonings from package. Make 4 ½-inch-deep slits about 4 inches apart. Insert a garlic sliver in each slit. Pour water and wine over brisket. Cover. Microwave on HIGH 15 minutes, rotating the casserole after 15 minutes. Turn meat over and rotate the casserole. Add potatoes, onions, carrots, and cabbage. Cover. Microwave on MEDIUM 1 hour or until corned beef and vegetables are tender. Let stand, covered, 15 minutes before serving.

Easy Beef Stroganoff

Makes 4 servings   Cooking Time: 11½ to 13½ minutes

2 tablespoons butter
1 medium onion, chopped
8 ounces fresh mushrooms, chopped
¾ cup beef broth
2 tablespoons tomato paste
1 teaspoon Worcestershire sauce

1 teaspoon prepared mustard
½ teaspoon salt
¼ teaspoon black pepper
1 pound cooked beef, cut in julienne strips
1 cup dairy sour cream
Hot cooked noodles

In a 3-quart microsafe casserole, place butter. Microwave on HIGH 20 to 30 seconds or until butter melts. Add onion and mushrooms. Microwave on HIGH 3 minutes, stirring after 1½ minutes. Add broth, tomato paste, Worcestershire sauce, mustard, salt, pepper, and beef; blend well. Cover. Microwave on MEDIUM 8 to 10 minutes or until hot. Gradually stir in sour cream. Serve over hot noodles. To reheat, microwave on LOW. Do not boil.

Manicotti Crepes

Makes 6 servings   Cooking Time: 36 to 50 minutes

½ **pound lean ground beef**
½ **pound bulk Italian sausage**
⅓ **cup minced onion**
2 **eggs**
¼ **cup grated Parmesan cheese**
¼ **teaspoon salt**

1 **package (10 ounces) frozen chopped spinach, cooked and squeezed dry**
12 **crepes (6 inches diameter)**
2 **cups Herb Tomato Sauce (recipe on page 60)**
4 **ounces brick cheese, shredded (1 cup)**

In a 2-quart microsafe casserole, crumble ground beef and Italian sausage. Add onion. Cover. Microwave on HIGH 10 to 12 minutes or until beef is no longer pink, stirring every 2 minutes and breaking up beef; drain fat. Cover tightly with plastic wrap; set aside. In a medium bowl, beat eggs, Parmesan cheese, and salt. Add meat mixture and spinach; blend well. Place about ⅓ cup filling in the center of each crepe. Fold sides in and roll up. Spread about ¼ cup Herb Tomato Sauce over bottom of an 11 x 7-inch microsafe baking dish. Place 6 filled crepes, seam side down, in the baking dish. Spoon 2 tablespoons sauce over each filled crepe. Cover with vented plastic wrap. Repeat with remaining crepes in a separate 11 x 7-inch baking dish. Microwave 1 baking dish at a time on HIGH 7 to 10 minutes or until heated through, rotating the baking dish every 4 minutes. Sprinkle ½ cup shredded cheese evenly over crepes. Cover with plastic wrap. Microwave on MEDIUM 1 to 3 minutes or until cheese melts; set aside. Repeat with remaining crepes.

Classic Pot Roast

Makes 6 servings   Cooking Time: about 1 hour 33 minutes

1 **beef chuck roast (2½ to 3 pounds), fat trimmed**
1 **medium onion, chopped**
1 **can (10¾ ounces) cream of onion soup, undiluted**
¼ **cup Burgundy wine**
1 **teaspoon Worcestershire sauce**

½ **teaspoon salt**
⅛ **teaspoon black pepper**
2 **carrots, peeled and quartered**
2 **potatoes, peeled and quartered**
1 **tablespoon cornstarch**
2 **tablespoons water**

Use a fork to pierce roast well on both sides. In a 2½-quart microsafe casserole, place roast. In a small bowl, combine onion, soup, wine, Worcestershire sauce, salt, and pepper; blend well. Pour over meat. Cover. Microwave on MEDIUM 35 minutes. Turn roast over. Arrange carrots and potatoes around roast. Cover. Microwave on MEDIUM 45 minutes or until roast is tender, rotating the dish every 15 minutes. Remove roast and vegetables to a serving platter. Cover with aluminum foil; let stand, covered, 10 minutes. Blend cornstarch with water; stir into pan juices. Microwave on MEDIUM 3 minutes or until thickened, stirring after 1½ minutes. Serve gravy with roast.

GIFTS FROM THE SEA

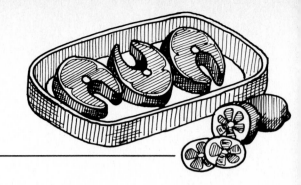

Fish Plaki

Makes 2 servings

Cooking Time: 11 to 15 minutes

1 cup chopped celery
½ cup chopped onion
¼ cup chopped carrot
3 tablespoons olive oil
1 can (16 ounces) whole tomatoes cut up; reserve juice
2 tablespoons tomato sauce
¼ cup chopped parsley

½ teaspoon salt
⅛ teaspoon white pepper
⅛ teaspoon garlic powder
2 fresh *or* thawed frozen halibut steaks, (about 1 pound)
2 tablespoons lemon juice
4 thin lemon slices

In a 2-quart microsafe bowl, combine celery, onion, carrot, and olive oil. Microwave on HIGH 4 to 7 minutes or until vegetables are tender, stirring every 2 minutes. Stir in tomatoes and juice, tomato sauce, parsley, salt, pepper, and garlic powder. Arrange steaks in a 12-inch microsafe oval baking dish. Sprinkle on lemon juice. Pour sauce over steaks. Arrange lemon slices on top. Microwave on HIGH 7 to 8 minutes or until fish flakes easily, rotating the baking dish once after 3 minutes.

Poached Fish Fillets

Makes 4 servings

Cooking Time: 12 to 15 minutes

4 fresh *or* thawed frozen fish fillets, such as flounder, sole, cod, *or* haddock (about 1½ pounds)
½ cup dry white wine
¼ cup water
3 thin lemon slices

1 small onion, sliced
Leaves from 2 ribs celery
1 bay leaf
½ teaspoon seasoned salt
⅛ teaspoon white pepper
Tartar Sauce

In a 12 x 7-inch microsafe baking dish, place fish fillets. Pour wine and water over fish. Arrange lemon slices on fillets. Add onion, celery leaves, bay leaf, salt, and pepper. Cover with plastic wrap. Microwave on HIGH 7 to 10 minutes or until fish flakes easily, rotating the baking dish every 3 minutes. Let stand, covered, 5 minutes. Use a slotted spoon to carefully remove fish from liquid. Lightly sprinkle paprika on fish. Serve with Tartar Sauce.

Tartar Sauce

Makes about 1½ cups

1 cup mayonnaise
½ cup sweet pickle relish, drained
2 teaspoons instant minced onion

1 teaspoon white vinegar
¼ teaspoon sugar

In a small bowl, combine all ingredients; blend well.

FISH/SEAFOOD

Confetti Tuna

Makes 4 servings   Cooking Time: 29¾ to 37¾ minutes

- 6 cups hot water
- 2 teaspoons vegetable oil
- ¼ teaspoon salt
- 4 ounces egg noodles
- 1 package (8 ounces) cream cheese
- 1 can (10¾ ounces) cream of celery soup, undiluted
- ½ cup chopped celery
- ¼ cup sliced green onion
- 2 cans (6½ ounces each) tuna, drained and flaked
- ¼ cup chopped drained pimiento

In a 4-quart microsafe casserole, combine water, oil, and salt. Cover. Microwave on HIGH 8 to 10 minutes or until boiling. Add noodles. Cover. Microwave on MEDIUM 12 to 15 minutes or until noodles are tender, stirring every 4 minutes; drain; set aside. In a large bowl, place cream cheese. Microwave on HIGH 45 seconds or until softened. Blend in soup, celery, and green onion. Cover. Microwave on HIGH 4 to 5 minutes or until hot, stirring every 2 minutes. Fold in noodles, tuna, and pimiento. Pour into a 12 x 7-inch microsafe baking dish. Cover with vented plastic wrap. Microwave on HIGH 5 to 7 minutes or until heated through, stirring after 2 minutes.

Seafood Shells

Makes 4 servings   Cooking Time: 18 to 24 minutes

- 12 jumbo macaroni shells, cooked and drained
- 3 tablespoons butter
- 8 ounces fresh mushrooms, sliced
- 1 tablespoon cornstarch
- 1 cup milk
- 1 cup half-and-half
- ¼ teaspoon salt
- ⅛ teaspoon white pepper
- 2 egg yolks, slightly beaten
- 2 tablespoons dry sherry
- ¼ teaspoon Worcestershire sauce
- 1 package (6 ounces) frozen crab meat, thawed, drained, and flaked
- 5 ounces small frozen shrimp, thawed
- 2 tablespoons chopped drained pimiento
  Grated Parmesan cheese
  Minced parsley
  Pimiento strips

Cover shells to prevent drying while making sauce. In a 1-quart microsafe casserole, place butter. Microwave on HIGH 20 to 30 seconds or until butter melts. Add mushrooms. Microwave on HIGH 4½ to 5½ minutes or until tender, stirring every 2 minutes. Use a slotted spoon to remove mushrooms from butter; set aside. Stir cornstarch into butter. Slowly stir in milk, half-and-half, salt, and pepper. Microwave on HIGH 6 to 8 minutes or until bubbly and thickened, stirring every 2 minutes. Blend ½ cup white sauce into egg yolks. Slowly return egg yolk mixture to white sauce. Stir in sherry and Worcestershire sauce. Microwave on MEDIUM 2 to 3 minutes or until bubbly and thickened. In a medium bowl, combine crab meat, shrimp, mushrooms, chopped pimiento, and ¾ cup sauce; stuff shells with seafood mixture. Pour remaining sauce into a 12 x 7-inch microsafe baking dish. Arrange filled shells in the baking dish. Spoon a small amount of sauce over each shell. Cover with vented plastic wrap. Microwave on MEDIUM 5 to 7 minutes or until heated through, rotating the baking dish every 2 minutes. Sprinkle on Parmesan cheese and minced parsley. Garnish with pimiento strips.

Spaghetti with Clam Sauce

Makes 4 servings   Cooking Time: 27 to 33 minutes

- 6 cups hot water
- 1 tablespoon vegetable oil
- ¼ teaspoon salt
- ½ pound uncooked spaghetti, broken in half
- 5 tablespoons butter, divided
- ¼ cup minced green onion
- 1 small clove garlic, pressed or minced

- 2 cans (8 ounces each) minced clams with juice
- ¼ cup dry white wine
- 1 teaspoon cornstarch
- 1 tablespoon minced parsley
- ⅛ teaspoon white pepper
  Grated Parmesan cheese

In a 3-quart microsafe casserole, combine water, oil, and salt. Cover. Microwave on HIGH 10 minutes or until boiling. Add spaghetti, covering with water. Microwave on MEDIUM 12 to 14 minutes or until spaghetti is tender, stirring every 3 minutes. Drain; rinse with hot water. Place on a warm serving platter; cover with aluminum foil; set aside. In a 3-quart microsafe casserole, place 4 tablespoons butter, onion, and garlic. Microwave on HIGH 3 to 5 minutes or until onion is tender. Drain clam juice into onion mixture. Stir in clams, wine, cornstarch, parsley, pepper. and remaining 1 tablespoon butter. Microwave on MEDIUM 2 to 4 minutes or until heated through. Pour clam sauce over spaghetti; toss to coat. Sprinkle Parmesan cheese on top and serve immediately.

Salmon Pie

Makes 4 to 5 servings   Cooking Time: 15 to 16 minutes

- ¾ cup coarse cracker crumbs, divided
- 1 can (15 ounces) red or pink salmon, skinned and flaked
- 2 tablespoons lemon juice
- 1 can (16 ounces) whole kernel corn, drained
- 1 cup milk
- 2 eggs, slightly beaten

- 2 tablespoons minced parsley
- 2 tablespoons instant minced onion
- ½ teaspoon Worcestershire sauce
- ¼ teaspoon dry mustard
- ⅛ teaspoon white pepper
- 4 ounces Cheddar cheese, shredded (1 cup)

Into a 9-inch microsafe pie plate, sprinkle ¼ cup cracker crumbs. Spread salmon around the edge of the plate. Sprinkle lemon juice on salmon. Cover the center of the pie plate with corn. In a medium bowl, combine remaining ½ cup crumbs, milk, eggs, parsley, onion, Worcestershire sauce, dry mustard, and pepper; blend well. Spoon about ¼ cup crumb mixture over corn and remaining mixture over salmon. Cover with plastic wrap. Microwave on HIGH 8 to 9 minutes or until hot. Let stand, covered, 5 minutes. Sprinkle cheese over pie. Cover with plastic wrap. Microwave on MEDIUM 2 minutes or until cheese melts.

Coquilles Saint Jacques

Makes 4 servings   Cooking Time: 12 to 15 minutes

1 pound fresh *or* thawed frozen scallops
3 tablespoons butter
1½ cups sliced fresh mushrooms
2 tablespoons minced onion
1 clove garlic, pressed or minced

⅓ cup dry white wine
1 tablespoon minced parsley
½ teaspoon salt
Cream Sauce
Paprika

If scallops are large, cut in halves or quarters; set aside. In a 2-quart microsafe casserole, combine butter, mushrooms, onion, and garlic. Microwave on HIGH 3 to 4 minutes or until mushrooms are tender. Stir in scallops, wine, parsley, and salt. Microwave on HIGH 4 minutes, stirring after 2 minutes. Drain liquid; reserve ½ cup for Cream Sauce. Prepare Cream Sauce. Stir sauce into scallop mixture. Spoon into 4 ramekins or small bowls. Microwave on MEDIUM 5 to 7 minutes or until heated through, rearranging every 2 minutes. (Do not overcook.) Sprinkle on paprika and serve.

Cream Sauce

Makes about 1¼ cups   Cooking Time: 3½ to 4½ minutes

3 tablespoons butter
2 tablespoons flour
½ cup half-and-half

½ cup reserved scallop cooking liquid

In a 1-quart glass measure, place butter. Microwave on HIGH 30 to 40 seconds or until butter melts. Blend in flour. Stir in scallop cooking liquid and half-and-half. Microwave on MEDIUM 3 to 4 minutes or until thickened, stirring every 1 minute.

Shrimp Quiche

Makes 4 servings   Cooking Time: 32 to 37½ minutes

6 ounces American cheese, coarsely chopped
1 baked 9-inch Basic Piecrust, cooled (recipe on page 64)
1½ cups frozen cooked small shrimp, thawed
¼ cup chopped celery

¼ cup thinly sliced green onion
1 tablespoon butter
1 cup half-and-half
½ teaspoon salt
½ teaspoon crushed leaf tarragon
¼ teaspoon black pepper
4 eggs, slightly beaten

Sprinkle cheese in piecrust; set aside. In a 1-quart microsafe casserole, combine shrimp, celery, onion, and butter. Cover. Microwave on HIGH 3 to 4 minutes or until onion is tender; drain well. Sprinkle shrimp mixture over cheese. In a 1-quart glass measure, combine half-and-half, salt, tarragon, and pepper. Microwave on HIGH 2 to 3½ minutes or until almost boiling. Gradually stir half-and-half mixture into eggs. Pour egg mixture into piecrust. Microwave on MEDIUM 17 to 20 minutes or until a knife inserted near the center comes out clean, rotating the dish every 5 minutes. (The center should be almost set.) Let stand 10 minutes before serving.

FROM THE DAIRY CASE

Crustless Broccoli Quiche

Makes 4 servings

Cooking Time: 21 to 23 minutes

- 2 tablespoons dry bread crumbs
- 3 ounces Swiss cheese, shredded (¾ cup)
- 3 ounces Monterey Jack cheese, shredded (¾ cup)
- 3 eggs
- 1 cup half-and-half

- 1 package (10 ounces) frozen chopped broccoli, cooked and drained
- 1 can (4 ounces) sliced mushrooms, drained
- 2 tablespoons minced green onion
- ½ teaspoon salt
- ¼ teaspoon white pepper

Butter an 8 or 9-inch microsafe quiche dish. Sprinkle crumbs over the bottom. Sprinkle both cheeses over crumbs. In a 2-quart microsafe bowl, beat eggs until blended. Stir in half-and-half, broccoli, mushrooms, onion, salt, and pepper. Pour into the quiche dish. Microwave on MEDIUM 5 minutes, rotating the quiche dish every 2 minutes and stirring the outside edge toward the center, spreading evenly in pie shell. Microwave on MEDIUM 9 to 11 minutes or until set, rotating the quiche dish every 3 minutes. Let stand 7 minutes before serving.

Hacienda Frittata

Makes 4 servings

Cooking Time: about 27 minutes

- 2 tablespoons butter
- 1 cup southern-style frozen hashed brown potatoes
- 1 cup sliced fresh mushrooms
- 2 cups thinly sliced and quartered zucchini
- ¼ cup chopped onion
- 8 eggs

- 2 tablespoons milk
- ½ teaspoon salt
- ½ teaspoon hot pepper sauce
- ⅓ cup shredded Cheddar cheese, room temperature
- ⅔ cup dairy sour cream
- ½ cup taco sauce

Preheat a 10-inch microwave browning dish on HIGH 5 minutes. Place butter in the dish; spread over the bottom. Add potatoes, mushrooms, zucchini, and onion. Microwave on HIGH 8 minutes or until vegetables are almost tender, rotating the dish every 2 minutes and stirring. In a medium bowl, beat eggs, milk, salt, and hot pepper sauce. Remove the browning dish from oven. Pour egg mixture over vegetables. Microwave on MEDIUM 12 minutes, rotating the dish every 3 minutes and stirring the outside edge toward the center. Sprinkle cheese over eggs. Cover tightly with plastic wrap; let stand 2 minutes. Spoon sour cream over the top. Spoon taco sauce over sour cream and serve.

Onion-Bacon Quiche

Makes 4 to 6 servings   Cooking Time: 36 to 41 minutes

¾ pound thinly sliced bacon
1 baked Basic Piecrust (recipe on page 64)
3 eggs
1 cup half-and-half

¼ teaspoon nutmeg
   Dash cayenne pepper
4 ounces Swiss cheese, shredded (1 cup)
½ cup finely chopped green onions

In an 11 x 7-inch paper towel-lined microsafe baking dish, place 4 to 5 strips bacon. Do not overlap. Cover with a paper towel. Place 4 to 5 more strips bacon on the paper towel. Cover with a paper towel. Repeat until all strips are used. Microwave on HIGH 12 to 15 minutes or until bacon is crisp, rotating the baking dish every 3 minutes. Immediately remove bacon from paper towels. Drain on paper towel-lined plate. Crumble bacon into piecrust. In a small bowl, beat eggs, half-and-half, nutmeg, and pepper until blended. Sprinkle cheese and onions over bacon. Pour egg mixture into piecrust. Microwave on MEDIUM 10 minutes, rotating the pie plate every 2 minutes and stirring the outside edge of mixture toward the center, spreading evenly in piecrust. Microwave on MEDIUM 9 to 11 minutes or until set, rotating the pie plate every 3 minutes. Let stand 5 minutes before serving.

Western Omelet

Makes 2 servings   Cooking Time: 9 to 11½ minutes

2 tablespoons butter
½ cup diced cooked ham
¼ cup chopped green onion
⅓ cup thinly sliced fresh mushrooms
¼ teaspoon hot pepper sauce

4 eggs, well beaten
1 ounce Cheddar cheese, shredded (¼ cup)
1 small tomato, chopped
   Salt and pepper

In a 1½-quart microsafe casserole, place butter. Microwave on HIGH 20 to 30 seconds or until butter melts. Add ham, onion, mushrooms, and hot pepper sauce; blend well. Microwave on HIGH 3½ to 4½ minutes or until vegetables are tender, stirring every 1 minute. Pour eggs over the vegetable mixture. Microwave on MEDIUM 4 to 5½ minutes or until eggs are almost set, stirring the outside edge toward the center every 1½ minutes. Turn onto a serving dish. Top with cheese and tomato. Season with salt and pepper to taste. Let stand 1 minute before serving.

Creamy Egg Scramble

Makes 2 servings   Cooking Time: 6 to 7 minutes

- 1 package (3 ounces) cream cheese
- 2 tablespoons milk
- 3 eggs
- 1 teaspoon snipped chives
- 1 tablespoon butter
- Salt and pepper

In a small microsafe bowl, place cream cheese. Microwave on HIGH 30 to 40 seconds or until cream cheese softens; transfer to a mixer bowl. Add milk, eggs, and chives; beat with electric mixer until smooth. In a 9-inch microsafe pie plate, place butter. Microwave on HIGH 20 to 30 seconds or until butter melts; spread over the bottom of the pie plate. Pour in egg mixture. Microwave on MEDIUM 4 to 5½ minutes or until almost set, stirring the outside edge toward the center every 2 minutes. Let stand 1 minute or until set. Season with salt and pepper to taste.

Creole Cheese Soufflé

Makes 4 servings   Cooking Time: 20 to 24½ minutes

- Creole Sauce
- ¼ cup flour
- ½ teaspoon salt
- ¼ teaspoon paprika
- ⅛ teaspoon dry mustard
- Dash cayenne pepper
- 1 can (13 ounces) evaporated milk
- 6 ounces sharp Cheddar cheese, shredded (1½ cups)
- 2 tablespoons grated Parmesan cheese
- 5 jumbo eggs, separated, room temperature
- 1 teaspoon cream of tartar

Prepare Creole Sauce; set aside and keep warm. In a 1½-quart microsafe bowl, combine flour, salt, paprika, dry mustard, and cayenne pepper. Blend in milk. Microwave on HIGH 4 to 5 minutes or until thickened, stirring every 1 minute. Stir in both cheeses. Microwave on MEDIUM 1 to 1½ minutes or until cheese melts; blend well. Beat egg yolks with a wire whisk until well blended. Stir about ½ cup cheese sauce into beaten yolks; blend well. Stir remaining cheese sauce into yolk mixture; set aside. In a large mixing bowl, beat egg whites and cream of tartar until stiff but not dry. Do not overbeat. Stir about 1 cup of the egg whites into cheese sauce. Use a rubber spatula to fold in remaining egg whites until blended. Pour into a 2½-quart microsafe soufflé dish. Microwave on MEDIUM 10 minutes, rotating the dish after 5 minutes. Microwave on MEDIUM 5 to 8 minutes, rotating the dish every 2 minutes. Soufflé is done when it rises above the dish and is almost set. Serve immediately with Creole Sauce.

Creole Sauce

Makes about 1 cup   Cooking Time: 3 to 4 minutes

- 1 can (10¾ ounces) tomato soup, undiluted
- ¼ cup chopped pimiento-stuffed olives
- 1 tablespoon instant minced onion
- 1 tablespoon minced parsley
- 1 teaspoon butter
- ⅛ teaspoon garlic powder
- ⅛ teaspoon sugar
- Few drops hot pepper sauce

In a 1-quart microsafe bowl, combine all ingredients; blend well. Microwave on HIGH 3 to 4 minutes or until heated through, stirring every 1 minute.

ONE-DISH MAIN DISHES

Scalloped Ham

Makes 4 to 6 servings

Cooking Time: 15½ to 19½ minutes

3 tablespoons butter
½ cup chopped green pepper
2 tablespoons flour
½ teaspoon salt
½ teaspoon dry mustard
½ teaspoon Worcestershire sauce
2 drops hot pepper sauce

1¼ cups milk
1 ham slice, cut in 4 serving pieces (about 1 pound)
4 ounces sharp Cheddar cheese, shredded, (1 cup)
1 can (16 ounces) sliced potatoes, drained
1 jar (16 ounces) whole onions, drained

In a 1-quart glass measure, place butter. Microwave on HIGH 30 to 40 seconds or until butter melts. Stir in green pepper, flour, salt, mustard, Worcestershire and hot pepper sauces. Blend in milk. Microwave on HIGH 5 to 7 minutes or until thickened, stirring every 2 minutes. In the center of a 12 x 7-inch microsafe baking dish, place ham. Sprinkle cheese on top. Arrange potatoes along one side and onions along the other side of the ham. Pour sauce over casserole. Cover with waxed paper. Microwave on HIGH 10 to 12 minutes or until hot and bubbly, rotating the baking dish every 3½ minutes. Stir before serving.

Sloppy Joe Lasagna

Makes 4 servings

Cooking Time: 25 to 31 minutes

1 pound lean ground beef
1 cup chopped onions
½ cup chopped celery
¼ cup chopped green pepper
1 can (10¾ ounces) tomato soup, undiluted
1 teaspoon salt

¼ teaspoon black pepper
¼ teaspoon Worcestershire sauce
7 cooked lasagna noodles
3 ounces mozzarella cheese, shredded (¾ cup)
2 tablespoons grated Parmesan cheese

In a 2-quart microsafe casserole, combine ground beef, onions, celery, and green pepper. Microwave on HIGH 8 to 10 minutes or until beef is no longer pink, stirring every 3 minutes and breaking up beef; drain fat. Stir in soup, salt, pepper, and Worcestershire sauce. Microwave on HIGH 4 to 6 minutes or until vegetables are tender, stirring every 2 minutes. In a 12 x 7-inch microsafe baking dish, layer half of the following in order: lasagna noodles, meat mixture, and mozzarella cheese. Repeat with remaining half of ingredients. Sprinkle Parmesan cheese evenly over top. Cover with waxed paper. Microwave on MEDIUM 8 to 10 minutes or until bubbly, rotating the baking dish every 3 minutes. Let stand, covered, 5 minutes before serving.

Campers' Sausage Stew

Makes 6 servings   Cooking Time: 17 to 20 minutes

- 1 box (7 ounces) elbow macaroni, cooked and drained
- 1 pound precooked link sausage, cut diagonally in 1-inch pieces
- 1 cup tomato sauce
- 2 tablespoons instant minced onion, rehydrated
- ¼ cup parsley flakes
- 1 teaspoon salt
- ⅛ teaspoon black pepper
- 4 ounces Cheddar cheese, shredded (1 cup)
- 2 tablespoons butter

In a 12-inch microsafe oval baking dish, combine macaroni, sausage, tomato sauce, onion, parsley flakes, salt, and pepper. Cover with vented plastic wrap. Microwave on HIGH 8 minutes. Stir. Cover with vented plastic. Microwave on HIGH 7 to 10 minutes or until heated through. In a small bowl, mix cheese and butter. Sprinkle over casserole. Microwave, uncovered, on MEDIUM 2 minutes or until cheese melts.

Potato Lasagna

Makes 4 servings   Cooking Time: 37 to 45 minutes

- 1 pound lean ground beef
- ½ cup chopped onion
- 1 clove garlic, minced
- 1 teaspoon salt
- ½ teaspoon black pepper
- 1 can (8 ounces) tomato sauce
- 1 cup water
- 2 tablespoons chopped parsley
- ½ teaspoon crushed leaf oregano
- 4 large potatoes, peeled and sliced crosswise thinly
- Grated Parmesan cheese

In a 2-quart microsafe baking dish, combine ground beef, onion, garlic, salt, and pepper. Microwave on HIGH 4 to 6 minutes or until beef is no longer pink, stirring every 1½ minutes and breaking up beef; drain fat. Stir in tomato sauce, water, parsley, and oregano. Microwave on HIGH 3 to 4 minutes or until hot. In the bottom of a 12-inch oval or 12 x 9-inch rectangular microsafe baking dish, arrange half of potatoes. Spoon half of meat mixture over potatoes; cover with remaining potatoes and meat. Cover with plastic wrap. Microwave on HIGH 20 to 25 minutes or until potatoes are tender, rotating the baking dish every 5 minutes. Sprinkle on Parmesan cheese. Cover tightly with aluminum foil. Let stand 10 minutes before serving.

CASEROLES

Broccoli-Ham Divan

Makes 4 servings

Cooking Time: 23 to 27 minutes

1½ pounds fresh broccoli spears, washed and drained
¼ cup water
1 ham slice (about 1 pound)
1 can (10¾ ounces) cream of celery soup, undiluted
¼ cup milk

1 can (8 ounces) mushroom stems and pieces, drained
1 teaspoon Dijon mustard
1 teaspoon horseradish
4 ounces Cheddar cheese, shredded (1 cup)

Cut broccoli into flowerets leaving 2-inch stems. In a 12-inch microsafe oval baking dish, arrange broccoli with stems toward the outside of the dish. Add water. Cover with vented plastic wrap. Microwave on HIGH 10 to 12 minutes or until tender, rotating the baking dish every 4 minutes; drain. Arrange ham over broccoli toward the edge of the dish. In a medium bowl, combine soup, milk, mushrooms, mustard, and horseradish; blend well; pour over ham. Cover with vented plastic wrap. Microwave on MEDIUM 10 to 12 minutes or until bubbly, rotating the baking dish every 3 minutes. Sprinkle cheese over top. Cover with vented plastic wrap. Microwave on MEDIUM 2 minutes or until cheese melts. Let stand, covered, 1 minute before serving.

Turkey-in-a-Hurry

Makes 4 to 5 servings

Cooking Time: 13 to 16 minutes

3 cups cubed cooked turkey
¼ cup chopped celery
¼ cup chopped onion
1 can (4 ounces) mushroom stems and pieces, drained

1 teaspoon parsley flakes
1 can (10¾ ounces) cream of mushroom soup, undiluted
½ cup milk
1½ cups seasoned croutons

In a 12 x 7-inch microsafe baking dish, combine all ingredients, except croutons. Cover tightly with plastic wrap. Microwave on HIGH 8 to 10 minutes, stirring every 3 minutes. Sprinkle croutons over top. Microwave, uncovered, on HIGH 2 to 3 minutes or until hot and bubbly. Let stand 3 minutes before serving.

Frankfurter Picnic

Makes 4 to 6 servings

Cooking Time: 11 to 14 minutes

2 cans (16 ounces each) pork and beans
1 pound frankfurters, cut diagonally in ½-inch pieces
½ cup chopped onion
½ cup catsup

¼ cup firmly packed light brown sugar
2 tablespoons prepared mustard
4 slices process American cheese, cut in strips

In a 2½-quart microsafe casserole, combine all ingredients except cheese. Cover. Microwave on HIGH 10 to 12 minutes or until bubbly, stirring every 3½ minutes. Arrange cheese slices over top. Cover. Microwave on MEDIUM 1 to 2 minutes or until cheese melts.

CASEROLES

Budget Beef Bake

Makes 6 servings

Cooking Time: 24½ to 28½ minutes

- 1 package (8 ounces) cream cheese
- 1 tablespoon snipped chives
- 1 pound lean ground beef
- ½ cup minced onion
- 1 box (7 ounces) elbow macaroni, cooked and drained
- 1 can (8 ounces) tomato sauce
- 1 teaspoon salt
- 1 teaspoon sugar
- ½ teaspoon crushed leaf basil
- ¼ teaspoon garlic powder
- ⅛ teaspoon black pepper
- 2 ounces Cheddar *or* brick cheese, shredded (½ cup)
- 6 pimiento-stuffed olives, sliced

In a small bowl, place cream cheese. Microwave on HIGH 20 to 25 seconds or until softened. Stir in chives; set aside. In a 2-quart microsafe casserole, combine ground beef and onion. Microwave on HIGH 8 to 10 minutes or until beef is no longer pink, stirring every 3 minutes and breaking up beef; drain fat. Add cream cheese mixture, macaroni, tomato sauce, salt, sugar, basil, garlic powder, and pepper; toss to coat well. Cover with waxed paper. Microwave on MEDIUM 6 minutes, stirring every 2 minutes. Cover with waxed paper. Microwave on MEDIUM 4 to 6 minutes or until hot and bubbly. Sprinkle Cheddar cheese over top. Microwave on MEDIUM, uncovered, 3 minutes or until heated through. Let stand 3 minutes before serving. Garnish with sliced olives.

Vegetarian Manicotti

Makes 4 servings

Cooking Time: 52 to 57 minutes

- 2 tablespoons butter
- ½ cup thinly sliced green onions
- 1 package (10 ounces) frozen chopped spinach, cooked and drained
- ½ cup small curd cottage cheese
- ½ cup ricotta cheese
- 2 tablespoons grated Parmesan cheese
- 1 teaspoon farina cereal
- 1 egg
- ¼ teaspoon salt
- ¼ teaspoon dillweed
- ⅛ teaspoon black pepper
  Dash garlic powder
- 8 uncooked manicotti tubes
- 2 cups Herb Tomato Sauce (recipe on page 60)
- 2½ cups hot water
  Grated Romano cheese

In a medium bowl, combine butter and onions. Microwave on HIGH 3 minutes, stirring every 1 minute. Add spinach, cottage, ricotta and Parmesan cheeses, farina, egg, salt, dillweed, pepper, and garlic powder; blend well. Fill manicotti tubes with spinach mixture. In a 2-quart microsafe bowl, combine Herb Tomato Sauce and water; blend well. Cover with vented plastic wrap. Microwave on HIGH 4 to 6 minutes or until hot. Pour half of sauce into a 12 x 7-inch microsafe baking dish. Arrange manicotti over sauce. Spoon remaining sauce over manicotti. Cover with vented plastic wrap. Microwave on HIGH 10 minutes, rotating the baking dish after 5 minutes. Turn each manicotti over; spoon sauce over top. Cover. Microwave on MEDIUM 15 minutes, rotating the baking dish every 4 minutes. Turn manicotti over; spoon sauce over top. Cover. Microwave on MEDIUM 5 to 8 minutes or until manicotti is tender. Let stand, covered, 15 minutes. Sprinkle on Romano cheese before serving.

GREAT GO-ALONGS

Sweet Yams 'n Ham

Makes 4 servings

Cooking Time: 7½ to 10 minutes

3 tablespoons butter
1 can (16 ounces) yams, drained
1 can (8 ounces) crushed pineapple, well drained; reserve 3 tablespoons juice
¼ cup chopped pecans
¼ cup crushed graham cracker crumbs

⅓ cup miniature marshmallows
2 tablespoons brown sugar
8 slices boiled ham (¼ inch thick)
8 pineapple chunks
8 maraschino cherries

In a 2-quart microsafe bowl, place butter. Microwave on HIGH 30 seconds or until butter melts. Add yams; mash well with a fork. Stir in pineapple, nuts, crumbs, marshmallows, and brown sugar. Divide mixture evenly among ham slices; spread over ham. Roll up, jelly-roll fashion. Secure with wooden picks if necessary. Place rolls, seam side down, in an 11 x 7-inch microsafe baking dish. Pour pineapple juice over rolls. Cover with vented plastic wrap. Microwave on HIGH 7 to 10 minutes or until hot, rotating the baking dish after 3 minutes. Spoon glaze over each roll. Garnish each with a pineapple chunk and a cherry and serve.

Zucchini and Tomatoes

Makes 4 servings

Cooking Time: 11 to 16½ minutes

2 tablespoons vegetable oil
½ cup chopped onion
1 clove garlic, pressed or minced
1 zucchini (about 1 pound), sliced crosswise ¼ inch thick (about 4 cups)

1 can (8 ounces) stewed tomatoes
½ teaspoon salt
⅛ teaspoon dried dillweed
⅛ teaspoon black pepper
⅛ teaspoon sugar

In a 2-quart microsafe casserole, combine oil, onion, and garlic. Cover. Microwave on HIGH 1 to 1½ minutes. Add remaining ingredients; stir to blend. Cover. Microwave on HIGH 10 to 15 minutes or until zucchini is tender, stirring every 4 minutes.

Stewed Okra

Makes 2 to 3 servings

Cooking Time: about 18 minutes

1 package (10 ounces) frozen cut okra
1 can (14½ ounces) stewed tomatoes; reserve juice
1 teaspoon lemon juice

¼ teaspoon salt
⅛ teaspoon crushed leaf oregano
Dash black pepper

In a 2-quart microsafe casserole, place okra. Cover. Microwave on HIGH 3 minutes. Stir to separate okra. Stir in tomatoes, lemon juice, salt, oregano, and pepper. Cover. Microwave on HIGH 10 minutes, stirring after 5 minutes. Microwave on HIGH 5 minutes or until okra is tender.

SIDE DISHES

Creamy Potato Salad

Makes 6 servings   Cooking Time: 17 to 22 minutes

6 medium potatoes, peeled and quartered
½ cup mayonnaise
¼ cup dairy sour cream
¼ cup grated carrot
⅓ cup sliced green onions
1 dill pickle, chopped
2 teaspoons cider vinegar
1¼ teaspoons salt

1 teaspoon prepared mustard
⅛ teaspoon black pepper
¾ cup thinly sliced celery
¼ cup minced green pepper
3 hard-cooked eggs, chopped
2 tablespoons minced parsley

In a 3-quart microsafe casserole, place potatoes. Add enough hot water to cover potatoes. Cover. Microwave on HIGH 15 to 20 minutes or until potatoes are tender, stirring every 8 minutes. Let stand, covered, 2 minutes. Drain and cool. Slice potatoes thinly. In a large bowl, combine mayonnaise, sour cream, carrot, green onions, dill pickle, vinegar, salt, mustard, and pepper; blend well. Add potatoes, celery, green pepper, and eggs; toss lightly to coat all vegetables. Sprinkle on parsley. Chill before serving.

Spinach Mountains

Makes 6 servings   Cooking Time: about 10 minutes

10 ounces spinach, washed and chopped
1 teaspoon salt
2 tablespoons dry bread crumbs
¼ cup sliced green onions
2 small eggs, slightly beaten
2 tablespoons melted butter

2 tablespoons grated Parmesan cheese
¼ teaspoon garlic salt
⅛ teaspoon crushed leaf oregano
⅛ teaspoon black pepper
6 tomato slices (½ inch thick)
Grated Parmesan cheese

In a colander, place spinach; sprinkle on salt. Let stand ½ hour. Place spinach in a 1-quart microsafe casserole. Cover. Microwave on HIGH 5 minutes; cool slightly and squeeze out excess moisture; return to casserole. Add bread crumbs, onions, eggs, butter, 2 tablespoons Parmesan cheese, garlic salt, oregano, and pepper; mix well. On a 12-inch microsafe plate, place tomato slices. Use an ice cream scoop to mound about ⅓ cup spinach mixture on top of each tomato slice. Microwave on HIGH 5 minutes. Sprinkle Parmesan cheese on top and serve.

Zucchini Coins

Makes 4 servings   Cooking Time: 8 to 10 minutes

1 zucchini squash (about 1 pound), sliced
    ¼ inch thick (4 cups)

1 tablespoon butter
⅓ cup grated Parmesan cheese

In an 8-inch microsafe baking dish, arrange a layer of zucchini slices. Dot with half the butter. Sprinkle on half the Parmesan cheese. Repeat with remaining zucchini, butter, and cheese. Cover with vented plastic wrap. Microwave on MEDIUM 8 to 10 minutes or until zucchini is tender, rotating the baking dish after 4 minutes.

SIDE DISHES

Vegetable Party Platter

Makes 6 to 8 servings   Cooking Time: 6 to 8 minutes

 6 fresh mushrooms with stems
 ¾ cup sliced zucchini (¼ inch thick)
 ¾ cup sliced yellow squash (¼ inch thick)
 1 small head cauliflower, broken into
     flowerets
 2 cups broccoli flowerets

 2 tablespoons butter
 2 tablespoons lemon juice
 7 cherry tomatoes
 7 sprigs parsley
     Hollandaise Sauce (recipe on page 59)

Remove the stem from 1 large mushroom. In the center of a 12-inch glass serving plate, place trimmed mushroom. Arrange remaining mushrooms with stems toward center of the plate. Arrange zucchini and yellow squash slices alternately in a circle around mushrooms. Place cauliflower and broccoli flowerets in 2 circles around squash, stems toward zucchini. In a 6-ounce custard cup, place butter. Microwave on HIGH 20 seconds or until butter melts. Stir in lemon juice. Drizzle over vegetables. Cover with vented plastic wrap. Microwave on HIGH 6 to 8 minutes or until vegetables are tender-crisp. Arrange cherry tomatoes and parsley between flowerets. Serve with Hollandaise Sauce.

Festive Rice Relish

Makes 4 to 5 servings

 1 cup prepared Long Grain Rice
 1 cup quartered, cooked artichoke hearts
 1 cup sliced fresh mushrooms
 1 green pepper, chopped
 2 pimientos, chopped

 1 large tomato, peeled and cubed
 2 tablespoons chopped onion
 2 tablespoons chopped parsley
     Vinaigrette

Prepare Long Grain Rice. In a medium bowl, combine all ingredients. Drizzle Vinaigrette over vegetable mixture; toss lightly. Chill before serving.

Long Grain Rice

Makes 4 servings   Cooking Time: about 29 minutes

 2¼ cups hot water
 1 tablespoon butter

 ¼ teaspoon salt
 1 cup long grain rice

In a deep 2-quart microsafe casserole, combine water, butter, and salt. Cover. Microwave on HIGH 4 to 5 minutes or until boiling. Stir in rice. Cover. Microwave on LOW 20 minutes or until rice is tender, stirring after 10 minutes. Let stand, covered, 5 minutes. Fluff with a fork.

Vinaigrette

 ⅔ cup olive oil
 ¼ cup white wine vinegar
 1 teaspoon salt

 ½ teaspoon white pepper
 1 clove garlic, pressed or minced

In a stoppered cruet or small bowl, combine all ingredients; shake or mix thoroughly.

Cabbage Patch

Makes 4 servings   Cooking Time: 17 to 19 minutes

4 cups shredded cabbage
1 medium onion, chopped
1 clove garlic, minced
1 cup water
3 tablespoons olive oil

¾ teaspoon salt
¼ teaspoon black pepper
1 can (8 ounces) tomato sauce
⅓ cup quick-cooking rice

In the bottom of a 12 x 7-inch baking dish, place cabbage. Add onion, garlic, water, oil, salt, pepper, and tomato sauce; mix lightly. Cover. Microwave on HIGH 7 minutes. Add rice; mix well. Cover. Microwave on HIGH 8 to 10 minutes or until cabbage is tender, stirring after 4 minutes. Let stand, covered, 2 minutes.

Salonika Salad

Makes 6 servings   Cooking Time: 17 to 22 minutes

6 medium potatoes, peeled and quartered
⅓ cup olive oil
½ cup thinly sliced green onions
3 tablespoons red wine vinegar

¼ cup minced parsley
1 teaspoon garlic salt
½ teaspoon crushed leaf oregano
⅛ teaspoon black pepper

In a 3-quart microsafe casserole, place potatoes. Add enough hot water to cover potatoes. Cover. Microwave on HIGH 15 to 20 minutes or until potatoes are tender, stirring every 8 minutes. Let stand, covered, 2 minutes. Drain and cool. Cut potatoes in large cubes. In a small bowl, combine remaining ingredients; blend well. Drizzle mixture over potatoes; toss lightly. Serve warm or chilled.

Wilted Lettuce Salad

Makes 6 servings   Cooking Time: 4½ to 6½ minutes

6 slices bacon
1 head leaf lettuce, torn into bite-size
    pieces (5 cups)
3 green onions, sliced
2 hard-cooked eggs, chopped
1 tomato, diced
2 radishes, sliced

¼ cup white wine vinegar
1 tablespoon sugar
2 tablespoons water
½ teaspoon salt
¼ teaspoon dry mustard
⅛ teaspoon black pepper

Place bacon on a microwave bacon rack. Cover with a paper towel. Microwave on HIGH 3½ to 4½ minutes or until crisp. Reserve 2 tablespoons drippings for dressing. Crumble bacon; set aside. In a salad bowl, combine lettuce, onions, eggs, tomato, and radishes. Cover and refrigerate until ready to serve. In a 1-cup glass measure, combine vinegar, bacon drippings, sugar, water, salt, mustard, and pepper. Microwave on HIGH 1 to 2 minutes or until boiling; stir to dissolve sugar. Drizzle over salad ingredients; toss lightly to coat. Sprinkle crumbled bacon on top.

SWEET AND SAVORY SAUCES

Medium White Sauce

Makes 2½ cups

Cooking Time: 6¼ to 7¼ minutes

- ¼ cup butter
- ¼ cup flour
- ¼ teaspoon salt
- ⅛ teaspoon white pepper
- 2 cups milk

In a 1-quart glass measure, place butter. Microwave on HIGH 45 seconds or until butter melts. Blend in flour, salt, and pepper to make a smooth paste. Microwave on HIGH 30 seconds. Use a wire whisk to blend in milk. Microwave on HIGH 5 to 6 minutes or until thick and smooth, whisking every 1 minute.

Variations

Thin White Sauce: Decrease butter and flour to 2 tablespoons each.

Thick White Sauce: Increase butter and flour to ½ cup each.

Herb White Sauce: Stir in ¼ teaspoon dried dillweed or basil.

Cheese Sauce

Makes about 1½ cups

Cooking Time: about 3½ minutes

- 2 tablespoons butter
- 2 tablespoons flour
- Dash white pepper
- 1 cup milk
- 4 ounces Cheddar cheese, shredded (1 cup)

In a 1-quart glass measure, place butter. Microwave on HIGH 20 to 30 seconds. Blend in flour and pepper. Gradually blend in milk. Microwave on HIGH 3 minutes or until bubbly and thickened, stirring every 1 minute. Add cheese; stir until cheese melts and sauce is smooth. If sauce cools before cheese melts, microwave on HIGH 15 to 20 seconds. Serve over vegetables.

Hollandaise Sauce

Makes about 1 cup

Cooking Time: about 1½ minutes

- ½ cup butter
- 2 tablespoons lemon juice
- 3 egg yolks, well beaten
- 2 tablespoons half-and-half
- Dash salt and white pepper

In a 2-cup glass measure, place butter. Microwave on HIGH 45 seconds or until butter melts. Stir in lemon juice, egg yolks, and half-and-half. Microwave on HIGH 50 to 60 seconds or until mixture begins to thicken, stirring every 20 seconds. Use a wire whisk to beat until smooth. Season with salt and pepper. Serve over vegetables or egg dishes.

SAUCES

Madeira Sauce

Makes about 1 cup   Cooking Time: 19 to 21 minutes

2 tablespoons butter *or* margarine
¼ cup finely chopped onion
¼ cup finely chopped celery
1 clove garlic, pressed or minced
1 tablespoon flour
1 cup chicken broth

1 teaspoon minced parsley
1 teaspoon tomato paste
⅛ teaspoon salt
¼ teaspoon crushed leaf thyme
⅛ teaspoon black pepper
½ cup Madeira wine

In a 1-quart microsafe mixing bowl, place butter. Microwave on HIGH 20 to 30 seconds or until butter melts. Add onion, celery, and garlic. Microwave on HIGH 5½ minutes or until bubbly, stirring every 2 minutes. Stir in flour. Microwave on HIGH 3 minutes or until flour browns, stirring after 1½ minutes. Stir in broth, parsley, tomato paste, salt, thyme, and pepper. Microwave on MEDIUM 8 to 10 minutes, stirring every 3 minutes. Use a sieve to strain sauce, pressing liquid from vegetables with a rubber spatula. Stir wine into strained sauce. Microwave on HIGH 2 minutes or until boiling. Serve hot over meat.

Herb Tomato Sauce

Makes about 2½ cups   Cooking Time: 8 to 10 minutes

1 can (15 ounces) tomato sauce
1 can (6 ounces) tomato paste
⅓ cup water
2 tablespoons grated Parmesan cheese
1 tablespoon minced parsley
1 teaspoon salt

1 teaspoon crushed leaf thyme
¾ teaspoon crushed leaf oregano
1 large clove garlic, pressed or minced
½ teaspoon sugar
¼ teaspoon black pepper

In a 2-quart microsafe casserole, combine all ingredients. Microwave on HIGH 8 to 10 minutes or until boiling, stirring every 2 minutes.

Swiss Cheese Sauce

Makes 1 cup   Cooking Time: 7½ to 8½ minutes

2 tablespoons butter
1 tablespoon cornstarch
¼ teaspoon salt
⅛ teaspoon white pepper

1 cup milk
4 ounces Swiss *or* Cheddar cheese, shredded (1 cup)

In a 1-quart glass measure, place butter. Microwave on HIGH 20 to 30 seconds or until butter melts. Blend in cornstarch, salt, and pepper to make a smooth paste. Microwave on HIGH 30 seconds. Use a wire whisk to blend in milk. Microwave on HIGH 6 to 8 minutes or until thickened, whisking every 2 minutes. Blend in cheese. Microwave on HIGH 30 seconds or until cheese melts; stir until smooth. Serve over vegetables.

Rum Raisin Sauce

Makes about 1¼ cups   Cooking Time: 10 to 12 minutes

1½ tablespoons cornstarch
¾ cup milk
1 cup firmly packed light brown sugar
¼ cup light corn syrup

2 tablespoons butter
½ cup raisins
2 tablespoons rum

In a 1-quart glass measure, dissolve cornstarch in milk. Add brown sugar, corn syrup, and butter. Microwave on HIGH 3 to 5 minutes or until thickened, stirring every 1 minute. Stir in raisins. Microwave on HIGH 2 minutes, stirring every 1 minute. Stir in rum. Let stand 5 minutes. Serve over ice cream or ham.

Chocolate Mallow Sauce

Makes about 2 cups   Cooking Time: 8½ to 12 minutes

½ cup firmly packed brown sugar
½ cup granulated sugar
½ cup water
½ cup milk

½ cup unsweetened cocoa
20 large marshmallows
1 teaspoon vanilla

In a 2-quart microsafe bowl, combine both sugars and water. Microwave on HIGH 7 to 10 minutes or until 220° F. on a candy thermometer, stirring every 3 minutes. Use a wire whisk to stir in milk and cocoa. Add marshmallows. Microwave on HIGH 1½ to 2 minutes or until marshmallows are puffy. Stir until marshmallows are completely melted. Blend in vanilla. Let stand to cool 30 minutes. Use a wire whisk to beat sauce until thick, about 5 minutes. Serve warm over ice cream or pound cake.

Berry Topping

Makes about 1⅓ cups   Cooking Time: 5 to 10 minutes

1 package (10 ounces) frozen raspberries
   or strawberries, partially thawed in
   package
2 teaspoons cornstarch

1 tablespoon water
2 teaspoons lemon juice
   Red food coloring, optional

In a 1-quart glass measure, empty package of partially thawed berries. Microwave on HIGH 2 to 3 minutes or until slightly icy, separating berries with a spoon; drain berries; reserve juice. In the same glass measure, dissolve cornstarch in water. Stir in reserved juice. Microwave on HIGH 1 to 2 minutes or until bubbly. Stir in berries. Microwave on HIGH 2 to 5 minutes or until clear and thickened, stirring every 1 minute. Stir in lemon juice and food coloring, if desired. Serve warm over ice cream or pound cake.

HAPPY ENDINGS

Grasshopper Pie

Makes 1 pie   Cooking Time: 3 to 5 minutes

36 large marshmallows
¼ cup milk
¼ cup creme de menthe
2 tablespoons white creme de cacao

2 cups whipping cream
Chocolate Cookie Crust, cooled
¼ cup chocolate cookie crumbs

In a 3-quart microsafe bowl, combine marshmallows and milk. Microwave on HIGH 3 to 5 minutes or until marshmallows melt, stirring every 1 minute. Stir in liqueurs. Chill 1 to 2 hours or until chilled, stirring 2 or 3 times. In a small mixing bowl, beat whipping cream with an electric mixer until stiff. Use a rubber spatula to fold whipped cream into marshmallow mixture. Pour into crust. Sprinkle cookie crumbs on top. Chill at least 3 hours or until set.

Chocolate Cookie Crust

Makes 1 piecrust   Cooking Time: 2¾ to 4 minutes

¼ cup butter
1⅓ cups finely crushed chocolate
    cookie crumbs

In a 9-inch microsafe pie plate, place butter. Microwave on HIGH 45 to 60 seconds or until butter melts. Blend in cookie crumbs. Press onto bottom and up sides of pie plate. Microwave on HIGH 2 to 3 minutes or until hot, rotating the pie plate every 1 minute. Cool before using.

Dreamy Peanut Pie

Makes 1 pie   Cooking Time: 6⅓ minutes to 8½ minutes

2 tablespoons butter
1½ cups creamy peanut butter, divided
1½ cups graham cracker crumbs
1 package (4¾ ounces) vanilla pudding
    and pie filling mix

2 cups milk
1 cup whipping cream
¼ cup sugar
Sweetened whipped cream

In a 9-inch microsafe pie plate, place butter. Microwave on HIGH 20 to 30 seconds or until butter melts. Add ½ cup peanut butter and the cracker crumbs to butter; blend well. Press crumb mixture onto bottom and up sides of the pie plate; set aside. In a 1-quart glass measure, combine pudding mix and milk. Microwave on HIGH 2 minutes; stir. Microwave on HIGH 4 to 6 minutes or until boiling and thickened, stirring every 1 minute. Blend in remaining 1 cup peanut butter. Chill thoroughly. In a small mixing bowl, beat whipping cream with an electric mixer until stiff, beating in sugar 1 tablespoon at a time. Use a rubber spatula to fold whipped cream into pudding mixture until no streaks of white remain. Pour into prepared piecrust. Chill at least 3 hours. Garnish with whipped cream.

PIES

Cheese-Topped Apple Pie

Makes 1 pie   Cooking Time: 17 to 20 minutes

- **4 cups peeled and thinly sliced apples**
- **½ cup sugar**
- **1 tablespoon lemon juice**
- **1 teaspoon cinnamon**
- **1 tablespoon cornstarch**

- **Basic Piecrust, cooled**
- **4 ounces Cheddar cheese, shredded (1 cup)**
- **Ice cream, optional**

In a large bowl, combine apples, sugar, lemon juice, cinnamon, and cornstarch; toss lightly to coat apples. Cover with waxed paper. Microwave on HIGH 6 to 8 minutes or until apples are tender, stirring gently every 3 minutes; set aside to cool slightly. Pour apple filling into piecrust. Sprinkle cheese on top. Microwave on MEDIUM 1 to 2 minutes or until cheese is almost melted. Let stand 10 minutes. Serve warm with ice cream, if desired.

Basic Piecrust

Makes 1 piecrust   Cooking Time: 5 to 7 minutes

- **3 tablespoons butter, room temperature**
- **1 cup flour**
- **¼ teaspoon salt**

- **1 to 3 tablespoons cold water**
- **1 egg yolk, well beaten**

In a large mixing bowl, place butter, flour, and salt. Use a pastry blender to cut butter into flour until particles resemble small peas. Sprinkle 1 tablespoon water at a time over flour mixture, blending until particles are moist enough to form a ball. Wrap dough in plastic wrap; chill 1 hour. Flatten dough to ½-inch thickness; roll out on a lightly floured pastry cloth to about a ⅛-inch-thick circle at least 2 inches larger than the inverted pie plate. Fit dough loosely into a 9-inch microsafe pie plate; let stand 10 minutes; flute the edges of the piecrust. Brush inside of the piecrust with egg yolk. Prick with a fork about ½ inch apart on bottom and sides. Microwave on HIGH 5 to 7 minutes or until golden, rotating the pie plate every 3 minutes. (If crust is cooking unevenly, rotate the pie plate ¼ turn every 1 minute. If crust bubbles, gently push it back into shape.)

Fruity Granola Pie

Makes 1 pie   Cooking Time: 10 to 18 minutes

- **1 can (21 ounces) apple *or* peach pie filling**
- **¼ cup golden raisins**
- **⅛ teaspoon cinnamon**
  Basic Piecrust (recipe above), cooled

- **1 cup crushed brown sugar and honey granola cereal**
- **1 tablespoon brandy**
  Ice cream

In a medium mixing bowl, combine pie filling, raisins, and cinnamon. Pour into piecrust. Sprinkle granola cereal evenly over pie. Drizzle brandy over granola. Microwave on HIGH 5 to 8 minutes or until bubbly and hot, rotating the dish every 2 minutes. Let stand 10 minutes before serving. Top with ice cream.

Banana Coconut Cream Pie

Makes 1 pie   Cooking Time: 16 to 22 minutes

¼ cup sugar
2 tablespoons plus 1 teaspoon cornstarch
2 tablespoons flour
Dash salt
2½ cups milk
2 egg yolks, slightly beaten
½ cup flaked coconut

½ teaspoon banana extract
Basic Piecrust (recipe on page 64), cooled
1 banana
Micro Meringue *or* **sweetened whipped cream**
Toasted Coconut, optional

In a 2-quart microsafe mixing bowl, combine sugar, cornstarch, flour, and salt; stir in milk. Microwave on HIGH 7 to 10 minutes or until bubbly and thickened, stirring with a wire whisk every 2 minutes. Stir about ½ cup milk mixture into egg yolks. Gradually return to milk mixture in bowl, stirring constantly. Microwave 1 to 2 minutes or until thickened, stirring with a wire whisk every 1 minute. Stir in coconut and banana extract. Cool slightly. Pour half of the filling into piecrust. Thinly slice banana; arrange on top of filling. Pour remaining filling over banana. Top with Micro Meringue, spreading to seal edges. Microwave on MEDIUM 8 to 10 minutes or until meringue is set. Garnish with Toasted Coconut, if desired.

Micro Meringue

3 egg whites
¼ teaspoon cream of tartar

6 tablespoons sugar
½ teaspoon vanilla

In a small mixing bowl, combine egg whites and cream of tartar. Beat with an electric mixer until soft peaks form. Add sugar, 1 tablespoon at a time, beating until stiff peaks form. Beat in vanilla. Spread over pie filling.

Toasted Coconut

2 tablespoons flaked coconut

Spread coconut in a 9-inch microsafe pie plate. Microwave on HIGH 2 minutes, stirring after 1 minute.

CAKES

Chocolate Snowcaps

Makes about 20

Cooking Time: 2½ to 3½ minutes

1 package (9 ounces) chocolate cake mix
½ cup sweetened condensed milk

½ cup flaked coconut
Confectioners' sugar

Cut lids from 2 styrofoam egg cartons (1 dozen each). Butter insides of egg holders. Prepare cake mix following package directions. Spoon 2 level tablespoonfuls into each egg compartment. Microwave on HIGH 2½ to 3½ minutes or until mixture bubbles and tops are slightly firm, rotating the carton after 1 minute. Let stand 2 minutes. Invert and gently push cakes out of carton onto a wire rack, separating if necessary. Let stand until cool. Dip the tops of cakes in sweetened condensed milk, then in coconut. Sprinkle confectioners' sugar on tops.

Boston Cream Pie

Makes 8 servings

Cooking Time: 16½ to 21 minutes

1 package (9 ounces) yellow cake mix
⅓ cup sugar
2 tablespoons cornstarch
1¼ cups milk

3 egg yolks, slightly beaten
1½ teaspoons vanilla
Chocolate Glaze

Prepare cake mix following package directions. Pour batter into a waxed paper-lined 8-inch round (2-quart) microsafe baking dish. Microwave on MEDIUM 6 minutes, rotating the baking dish every 2 minutes. Microwave on HIGH 3½ to 5 minutes or until the top of the cake is still slightly moist and a wooden pick inserted in the center comes out clean, rotating the baking dish every 1 minute. Use a knife to loosen the edge of the cake from the baking dish; invert onto a serving plate. Carefully peel waxed paper from cake. Let stand while preparing filling. In a 1-quart glass measure, combine sugar and cornstarch. Gradually stir in milk. Microwave on HIGH 2 minutes; stir. Microwave on HIGH 2 to 4 minutes or until very thick, stirring every 1 minute. Blend a little of the hot mixture into egg yolks. Gradually return egg yolk mixture to remaining milk mixture; blend well. Microwave on MEDIUM 3 to 4 minutes or until thick. Stir in vanilla. Cover with waxed paper; chill thoroughly. Slice cooled cake layer horizontally to make 2 thin layers. Spread filling on bottom layer. Top with second layer. Spread the top with Chocolate Glaze. Glaze will drizzle down the side of the cake. Chill until serving time.

Chocolate Glaze

Makes about 1 cup

Cooking Time: 2 to 3 minutes

2 tablespoons butter
½ cup semisweet chocolate chips

2 tablespoons milk
1 cup sifted confectioners' sugar

In a 1-quart glass measure, combine butter, chocolate chips, and milk. Microwave on HIGH 2 to 3 minutes or until chocolate melts; blend well. Use a wire whisk to stir in confectioners' sugar until smooth. If glaze thickens, beat in more milk.

CAKES

"Peach" of a Cake

Makes 6 to 8 servings

Cooking Time: 26 to 27½ minutes

2 tablespoons butter
¼ cup firmly packed light brown sugar
1 can (8 ounces) sliced peaches, drained; reserve syrup

½ cup crushed brown sugar and honey granola cereal
1 package (9 ounces) yellow cake mix
Ice cream

In an 8-inch round (2-quart) microsafe baking dish, place butter. Microwave on HIGH 20 to 30 seconds or until butter melts. Blend in brown sugar. Thinly slice peaches; arrange over brown sugar. Sprinkle cereal over peaches. Prepare cake mix following package directions, using reserved peach syrup for part of the liquid. Pour batter into the prepared baking dish, spreading evenly to cover peaches. Microwave on MEDIUM 6 minutes, rotating the baking dish every 2 minutes. Microwave on HIGH 3½ to 5 minutes or until a wooden pick inserted in the center comes out clean, rotating the baking dish every 2 minutes. Let stand 1 minute. Use a knife to loosen the edge of the cake from the baking dish; invert onto a serving plate. Let stand in the baking dish 10 minutes; remove the baking dish. Spread any topping remaining in the baking dish over cake. Let stand 5 minutes before serving with ice cream.

Choco-Mallow Cake

Makes 12 servings

Cooking Time: 16½ to 20½ minutes

2 squares (1 ounce each) unsweetened baking chocolate
½ cup butter
2 cups all-purpose flour
3 eggs, slightly beaten

½ cup semisweet chocolate chips
1 teaspoon vanilla
¼ teaspoon salt
½ cup flaked coconut
24 large marshmallows

Butter a 12 x 7-inch microsafe baking dish; set aside. In a 2-quart microsafe mixing bowl, combine chocolate squares, butter, and sugar. Microwave on HIGH 3 to 4 minutes or until chocolate melts, stirring every 1 minute; blend well. Add flour, eggs, chocolate chips, vanilla, and salt. Pour into the prepared baking dish. Shield corners of the baking dish with small pieces of aluminum foil. Place the baking dish on an inverted saucer in the oven. Microwave on MEDIUM 7 minutes, rotating the baking dish every 2½ minutes. Microwave on HIGH 3 to 5 minutes or until a wooden pick inserted near the center comes out clean, rotating the baking dish every 1½ minutes. Let stand to cool ½ hour. Sprinkle coconut on top. Arrange marshmallows evenly on top of coconut. Microwave on HIGH 3½ to 4½ minutes or until marshmallows are puffy. Use a spatula to swirl marshmallows, covering entire cake. Cut cake with a knife dipped in warm water.

Creme de Menthe Glaze

Makes ⅓ cup   Cooking Time: 3 to 3½ minutes

¾ cup milk chocolate chips   **1 teaspoon creme de menthe**
¼ cup dairy sour cream

In a small microsafe bowl, place chocolate chips. Microwave on MEDIUM 3 to 3½ minutes or until chips are shiny and smooth, stirring every 1 minute. Blend in sour cream, about 1½ tablespoons at a time. Stir in creme de menthe. Cool. Frosts the top and sides of a single 8-inch square or 9-inch round layer.

Nutty Coconut Frosting

Makes about 2 cups   Cooking Time: 4 to 6 minutes

1 cup evaporated milk   **1 teaspoon vanilla**
½ cup sugar   **1½ cups flaked coconut**
3 egg yolks, slightly beaten   **½ cup chopped nuts (walnuts, pecans,**
¼ cup butter   **   *or* almonds)**

In a 2-quart microsafe bowl, combine milk, sugar, egg yolks, butter, and vanilla. Microwave on HIGH 4 to 6 minutes or until thickened, stirring every 1 minute. Let stand until cool. Use a wire whisk to beat until thick and shiny. Stir in coconut and nuts. Frosts the tops and sides of 2 8-inch square or 9-inch round cake layers, a 12 x 8-inch sheet cake, or 24 cupcakes.

Vanilla Frosting

Makes about 2 cups   Cooking Time: 2½ minutes

1 box (1 pound) sifted confectioners'   **1 teaspoon vanilla**
**   sugar**   **¼ cup butter, sliced**
¼ cup milk *or* half-and-half   **2 to 3 teaspoons milk, optional**

In a large microsafe bowl, combine confectioners' sugar, milk, and vanilla. Place butter slices on top. Microwave on HIGH 2 minutes; stir. Microwave on HIGH 30 seconds; stir until smooth. Let stand until cool. Stir before using. For a creamier frosting, stir in milk. Frosts the tops and sides of 2 8-inch square or 9-inch round cake layers, a 12 x 8-inch sheet cake, or 24 cupcakes.

Variations

Coffee Frosting: Add ½ teaspoon instant coffee granules to butter mixture before cooking.

Butterscotch Frosting: Reduce vanilla to ½ teaspoon and add ¼ teaspoon butterscotch flavoring.

Peppermint Frosting: Substitute 1 teaspoon peppermint extract for the vanilla and add 2 drops red food coloring.

DESSERTS

Apple Crunch

Makes 8 servings

Cooking Time: 10 to 11 minutes

½ cup finely crushed cornflakes
¼ cup firmly packed brown sugar
¼ cup finely chopped walnuts
⅓ cup honey

4 large baking apples, peeled, cored
   and halved
Dairy sour cream

In a small bowl, combine cornflake crumbs, sugar, and nuts. Brush honey completely over apple halves. Roll apples in crumb mixture, coating well; gently press crumbs onto apples. Place in an 11 x 7-inch microsafe baking dish. Cover with vented plastic wrap. Microwave on HIGH 5 to 6 minutes, rotating the baking dish after 2½ minutes. Let stand 5 minutes. Top with dollops of sour cream and serve.

Peanut Caramel Shortcakes

Makes 6 servings

Cooking Time: 3 to 3½ minutes

½ pound caramels, unwrapped
½ cup milk
½ cup chopped roasted peanuts

6 scoops vanilla ice cream
6 dessert sponge cakes

In a 1-quart microsafe bowl, combine caramels and milk. Microwave on HIGH 3 to 3½ minutes or until caramels melt, stirring to blend. Stir in peanuts. Sauce can be served hot or at room temperature. Place 1 scoop ice cream in the center of each dessert cake. Pour about ⅓ cup sauce over ice cream.

Floating Islands

Makes 4 servings

Cooking Time: 13 to 18 minutes

2 eggs, separated, room temperature
⅓ cup sugar
2 teaspoons cornstarch
1½ cups milk

1 teaspoon vanilla, divided
4 tablespoons sugar
1 pint fresh strawberries, blueberries or
   raspberries

In a 2-quart microsafe bowl, combine egg yolks, sugar, and cornstarch; blend well. Gradually stir in milk. Microwave on MEDIUM 7 to 10 minutes or until boiling, stirring every 2 minutes. Microwave on MEDIUM 1 minute. Stir in ½ teaspoon vanilla. Refrigerate until ready to serve. Before serving, beat egg whites in a small mixing bowl with an electric mixer until soft peaks form. Beat in 4 tablespoons sugar, 1 tablespoon at a time, until stiff peaks form. Beat in remaining ½ teaspoon vanilla. Divide strawberries among 4 individual dessert dishes. Spoon chilled custard over berries. Divide meringue evenly on top of each custard. Microwave on MEDIUM 5 to 7 minutes or until meringue is set. Serve immediately.

DESSERTS

Bread Pudding

Makes 6 to 8 servings   Cooking Time: 25 to 34 minutes

2 cups milk
1 tablespoon butter
2 cups dry bread cubes
1½ tablespoons cornstarch
½ cup raisins
½ cup sugar

½ teaspoon cinnamon
1 teaspoon vanilla
¼ teaspoon salt
3 eggs, slightly beaten
Half-and-half

In a 1-quart glass measure, combine milk and butter. Microwave on HIGH 4 to 6 minutes or until hot but not boiling. In a 2½-quart microsafe bowl, combine bread cubes, cornstarch, raisins, sugar, cinnamon, vanilla, and salt. Gradually stir in milk. Blend in eggs. Microwave on HIGH 2 minutes; stir carefully. Microwave on MEDIUM 4 to 8 minutes or until almost set in the center, gently pushing the outer edge of pudding toward the center every 3 minutes. Do not overcook. Let stand 15 to 20 minutes. Serve warm or cold with half-and-half.

Mini Cherry Cheesecakes

Makes 6   Cooking Time: 5 to 6 minutes

1 package (8 ounces) cream cheese
½ cup sugar
2 eggs
2 teaspoons lemon juice

1 teaspoon vanilla
6 vanilla wafers
2 tablespoons dairy sour cream
2 tablespoons cherry preserves

In a medium microsafe bowl, place cream cheese. Microwave on MEDIUM 1 minute. Add sugar, eggs, lemon juice, and vanilla; beat with an electric mixer until light and fluffy. Place paper liners in muffin cups. Place 1 vanilla wafer in the bottom of each cup. Fill cups ⅔ full (about 3 tablespoons in each) with cheese mixture. Microwave on MEDIUM 4 to 6 minutes or until a knife inserted near the center comes out clean. Top each cheesecake with 1 teaspoon sour cream and 1 teaspoon cherry preserves. Chill before serving.

Favorite Brownies

Makes 28   Cooking Time: 13 to 22 minutes

**2 squares (1 ounce each) unsweetened
   baking chocolate**
½ cup butter
1 cup sugar
1 cup flour

3 eggs, slightly beaten
1 teaspoon vanilla
¼ teaspoon salt
½ cup finely chopped nuts

Butter a 12 x 7-inch microsafe baking dish; set aside. In a 2-quart microsafe bowl, combine chocolate, butter, and sugar. Microwave on HIGH 3 to 5 minutes or until chocolate and butter melt; blend well. Add remaining ingredients; mix well. Pour into the prepared baking dish. Place the baking dish on an inverted saucer in oven. Microwave on HIGH 5 to 7 minutes or until a wooden pick inserted near the center comes out clean, rotating the baking dish every 2 minutes. Let stand 5 to 10 minutes before cutting into bars.

Pineapple Noodle Kugel

Makes 8 servings

Cooking Time: 52 to 67½ minutes

6 cups hot water
1 tablespoon vegetable oil
¼ teaspoon salt
8 ounces medium egg noodles (4 cups)
3 eggs
¾ cup sugar
1 cup half-and-half

1 can (16 ounces) crushed pineapple, well drained
1 teaspoon grated lemon peel
½ cup butter
Dairy sour cream
Cinnamon

In a 4-quart microsafe casserole, combine hot water, oil, and salt. Cover. Microwave on HIGH 8 to 10 minutes or until boiling. Stir in noodles. Microwave on HIGH 2 to 4 minutes or until boiling. Microwave on MEDIUM 10 to 14 minutes or until noodles are tender but firm, stirring after 5 minutes; drain; set aside. In a large mixing bowl, beat eggs and sugar until thick and yellow. Stir in noodles, half-and-half, pineapple, and lemon peel; set aside. In a 12 x 7-inch microsafe baking dish, place butter. Microwave on HIGH 1 to 1½ minutes or until butter melts. Tilt dish to evenly coat with butter; pour excess into noodle mixture. Pour noodle mixture into buttered dish. Cover with vented plastic wrap. Microwave on MEDIUM 6 to 8 minutes, rotating the baking dish and stirring noodles from the outside edge toward the center every 3 minutes. Microwave on MEDIUM 10 to 15 minutes or until set, rotating the baking dish every 2 minutes. Let stand, covered, 15 minutes. Top with sour cream and cinnamon before serving.

Vanilla Pudding

Makes 4 servings

Cooking Time: 8 to 11 minutes

⅓ cup sugar
2 tablespoons cornstarch
1 tablespoon flour
⅛ teaspoon salt

2 cups milk
2 egg yolks, slightly beaten
1 teaspoon vanilla

In a 2-quart microsafe mixing bowl, combine sugar, cornstarch, flour, and salt. Stir in milk until smooth. Microwave on HIGH 7 to 10 minutes or until thickened and bubbly, stirring with a wire whisk every 2 minutes. Stir about ½ cup mixture into egg yolks. Return egg yolk mixture to milk mixture in bowl, stirring constantly. Microwave on HIGH 1 to 2 minutes or until thickened, stirring with a wire whisk every 1 minute. Stir in vanilla. Cover with waxed paper or plastic wrap placed directly on pudding to prevent a skin from forming. Cool slightly. Serve warm or cool.

Variations

Butterscotch Custard Pudding: Substitute firmly packed brown sugar for granulated sugar.

Coconut Custard Pudding: Stir ½ cup flaked coconut into mixture before cooking. Add ¼ teaspoon almond extract with the vanilla.

Fruit Compote

Makes 2 servings   Cooking Time: 6 to 7 minutes

2 medium apples, peeled, cored, and cubed
2 medium pears, peeled, cored, and cubed
3 tablespoons brown sugar
1 tablespoon honey

½ cup whole berry cranberry sauce
¼ teaspoon cinnamon
⅛ teaspoon ground cloves
Sweetened whipped cream

In a 1½-quart microsafe bowl, combine all ingredients, except whipped cream. Cover with waxed paper. Microwave on HIGH 3 minutes; stir. Microwave on HIGH 3 to 4 minutes or until fruit is tender. Cool slightly and serve topped with whipped cream.

Blueberry-Pears Flambé

Makes 4 servings   Cooking Time: 21½ to 24½ minutes

2 firm ripe pears
1 package (8 ounces) cream cheese
¼ cup finely chopped pecans
1 cup frozen blueberries, thawed

¾ cup sugar
3 tablespoons water
1 tablespoon cornstarch
2 tablespoons brandy, optional

Cut pears in half; core. In an 8-inch square baking dish, place pear halves, tops toward the middle of the dish. Cover with vented plastic wrap. Microwave on HIGH 4 to 5 minutes or until almost tender, rotating the baking dish after 2 minutes. Let stand, covered, 10 minutes. In a small microsafe bowl, place cream cheese. Microwave on MEDIUM 1 minute or until softened. Stir in pecans; set aside. In a 1-quart glass measure, combine blueberries, sugar, water, and cornstarch. Microwave on HIGH 6 to 8 minutes or until clear and thickened, stirring every 1 minute. Divide cheese mixture into 4 equal portions. Place in the centers of pears. Pour hot blueberry sauce over pears. Serve immediately. To flame, place brandy in a small microsafe dish. Microwave on HIGH 15 to 20 seconds to warm. Pour into ladle; ignite and pour into sauce. Pour flaming sauce over pears.

Chocolate Fondue

Makes about 1 cup   Cooking Time: 2½ to 4 minutes

1 package (6 ounces) semisweet chocolate chips
⅓ cup plus 1 tablespoon half-and-half
2 tablespoons butter
1 cup miniature marshmallows

2 tablespoons apricot brandy liqueur
Assortment of fruit, such as whole strawberries, orange sections, apple wedges, and pear wedges

In a 1-quart glass measure, combine first 4 ingredients. Microwave on HIGH 2½ to 4 minutes or until mixture thickens and comes to a full boil, stirring every 1 minute. Mixture should be thick and smooth. Stir in liqueur. If mixture is too thick, stir in a little more half-and-half. Serve warm with assorted fruit.

DESERTS

Fluffy Chocolate Cheesecake

Makes 1 pie

Cooking Time: 4 to 4½ minutes

- 1 package (8 ounces) cream cheese, room temperature
- 4 tablespoons butter *or* margarine, room temperature
- 2 teaspoons vanilla
- 1 package (12 ounces) semisweet chocolate chips

- 1 cup finely chopped walnuts
- 2 cups whipping cream, whipped
  Chocolate Cookie Crust (recipe on page 63)
  Chocolate curls, optional

In a 2-quart microsafe bowl, place cream cheese. Microwave on MEDIUM 20 to 25 seconds or until softened. Add butter; beat with electric mixer until smooth and creamy. Add vanilla; blend well; set aside. In a medium microsafe bowl, place chocolate chips. Microwave on MEDIUM 3½ to 4 minutes or until chocolate is shiny and smooth, stirring every 1 minute. Add melted chocolate and walnuts to cheese mixture; blend well. Use a rubber spatula to fold whipped cream into cheese mixture until no streaks of white remain. Pour into crust. Garnish with chocolate curls, if desired. Refrigerate 6 to 8 hours or until set.

Strawberry Clouds

Makes 3 servings

Cooking Time: 2½ to 3½ minutes

- 1 pint fresh strawberries, washed and hulled
  Strawberry Glaze
- 6 eggs, divided

- 3 tablespoons cream cheese, room temperature
  Sweetened whipped cream

Set aside ½ cup of the smaller berries for use in Strawberry Glaze. Prepare glaze; set aside. Break 2 eggs in each of 3 12-ounce custard cups; beat eggs well with a fork. Microwave on MEDIUM 1½ minutes; stir the outer edges toward the centers of the dishes. Microwave on MEDIUM 1 to 2 minutes or until eggs are set. Spread 1 tablespoon cream cheese over eggs in each cup. Spread 1½ tablespoons glaze over cream cheese. Divide and arrange remaining strawberries in each cup. Top each with 1½ tablespoons glaze. Garnish with dollops of whipped cream. Serve immediately.

Strawberry Glaze

Makes about 1 cup

Cooking Time: 5 to 7 minutes

- Reserved ½ cup strawberries
- ½ cup water

- ½ cup sugar
- 1½ tablespoons cornstarch

In a 1-quart glass measure, place reserved ½ cup strawberries; crush berries with a fork. Add water. Microwave on HIGH 2 to 3 minutes or until boiling. Into a 1-quart microsafe bowl, press berries through a sieve. Blend in sugar and cornstarch. Microwave on HIGH 3 to 4 minutes or until clear and thickened, stirring every 1 minute.

THE CONFECTIONARY

Peanut Brittle

Makes about ¾ pound   Cooking Time: 10 to 12 minutes

- **2 tablespoons butter**
- **⅓ cup sugar**
- **¼ cup molasses**

- **½ cup dark corn syrup**
- **1 cup salted roasted peanuts**
- **¼ teaspoon baking soda**

Butter a large baking sheet; set aside. In a 3-quart microsafe casserole, combine butter, sugar, molasses, and corn syrup. Microwave on HIGH 4 to 5 minutes or until sugar dissolves. Add peanuts. Microwave on HIGH 6 to 7 minutes or until mixture reaches the soft-crack stage (280° F.) on a microwave candy thermometer or when a little mixture dropped into cold water will separate into hard, but not brittle threads. Stir in baking soda. Pour onto the prepared baking sheet to cool and harden, about ½ to 1 hour. Break candy into irregular pieces. Store in an airtight container.

Divinity

Makes about 30 pieces   Cooking Time: 10 to 12 minutes

- **2 cups sugar**
- **⅓ cup light corn syrup**
- **½ cup water**
- **2 egg whites**

- **⅛ teaspoon salt**
- **1 teaspoon vanilla**
- **1 cup chopped walnuts**

In a 3-quart microsafe bowl, combine sugar, corn syrup, and water. Microwave on HIGH 3 minutes; stir. Microwave on HIGH 7 to 9 minutes or until 250° F. on a microwave candy thermometer. (Check temperature during last few minutes of cooking time.) In a small mixing bowl, beat egg whites and salt with an electric mixer until stiff. Slowly pour syrup mixture into egg whites in a thin stream, beating constantly with the mixer until mixture loses its shine and thickens. Stir in vanilla and nuts. Let stand until mixture holds its shape. Drop by teaspoonfuls onto waxed paper. Let stand overnight to set.

Candy Clusters

Makes about 3 dozen   Cooking Time: 3 to 4 minutes

- **1 package (6 ounces) semisweet chocolate chips**
- **3 tablespoons light corn syrup**
- **1 tablespoon water**

- **1 cup crisp cereal squares**
- **½ cup flaked coconut**
- **½ cup raisins**
- **½ cup butterscotch chips**

In a 1-quart microsafe bowl, combine chocolate chips, corn syrup, and water. Microwave on MEDIUM 3 to 4 minutes or until shiny and smooth, stirring every 1 minute. Stir in cereal, coconut, raisins, and butterscotch chips. Drop by rounded teaspoonfuls onto a waxed paper-lined baking sheet. Chill until firm.

Toffee Candy

Makes about 24 pieces

Cooking Time: about 6 to 8 minutes

- **7 tablespoons butter, divided**
- **10 graham cracker squares**
- **½ cup firmly packed brown sugar**
- **1 teaspoon vanilla**

- **½ cup sliced almonds *or* finely chopped nuts**
- **1 cup milk chocolate chips**

In an 11 x 7-inch baking dish, place 1 tablespoon butter. Microwave on HIGH 20 seconds; brush over bottom and sides of the baking dish. Line the bottom of the baking dish with graham cracker squares, cutting to fit the baking dish. In a 1-quart microsafe bowl, combine remaining 6 tablespoons butter and sugar. Microwave on HIGH 1 to 2 minutes or until butter melts. Add vanilla; beat with a wire whisk until smooth. Microwave on HIGH 2 minutes; stir. Pour over crackers; spread evenly. Sprinkle almonds on top. Microwave on HIGH 1½ to 3 minutes or until mixture boils, rotating the baking dish every 30 seconds. Microwave on HIGH 1 minute. Let stand 1 minute at room temperature. Sprinkle chocolate chips over top. Let stand until chocolate is softened; spread evenly. Loosen the edges; let stand until cool. Cut into quarters. Remove to a cutting surface; cut into small pieces. For crisp toffee, store in the refrigerator.

Ohio Buckeyes

Makes about 4 dozen

Cooking Time: 3½ to 6 minutes

- **1 cup margarine**
- **1 cup smooth peanut butter**
- **1 box (1 pound) sifted confectioners' sugar**

- **1 package (6 ounces) semisweet chocolate *or* butterscotch chips**

In a 3-quart microsafe bowl, combine margarine and peanut butter. Microwave on HIGH 2 to 3 minutes or until margarine melts. Add sugar; mix until smooth. Roll into 1-inch balls. Place on a waxed paper-lined baking sheet. Let stand at room temperature 2 to 3 hours or until firm. Place chocolate chips in a 1-quart glass measure. Microwave on HIGH 1½ to 3 minutes or until chips melt, stirring every 1 minute until shiny and smooth. Use a metal skewer to dip balls ¾ of the way into chocolate. Place on a waxed paper-lined baking sheet. Chill until firm.

Peppermint Bark

Makes about 2 pounds

Cooking Time: 3 to 4 minutes

- **1½ pounds white compound candy coating***

- **1 cup finely crushed peppermint candies**
- **¼ teaspoon peppermint extract**

Chop candy coating into small pieces. In a medium microsafe bowl, place candy coating. Microwave on MEDIUM 3 to 4 minutes, stirring every 1 minute until shiny and smooth. Add candies and peppermint extract, stirring constantly. Pour onto aluminum foil or waxed paper; spread to about ¼-inch thickness. Chill until firm. Break into pieces and store in an airtight waxed paper-lined container.

*Available where candymaking products are sold.

INDEX